Cards for
Tots to Teens

Over 60 fun designs for the children in your life

Marion Elliot

D&C
David and Charles

For Stella, with love from Mummy

A DAVID & CHARLES BOOK
Copyright © David & Charles Limited 2006

David & Charles is an F+W Publications Inc. company
4700 East Galbraith Road
Cincinnati, OH 45236

First published in the UK in 2006

Text and designs copyright © Marion Elliot 2006
Photography copyright © David & Charles Limited 2006

Marion Elliot has asserted her right to be identified as author of this work in accordance
with the Copyright, Designs and Patents Act, 1988.

A catalogue record for this book is available from the British Library.

ISBN-13: 978-0-7153-2581-0 hardback
ISBN-10: 0-7153-2581-7 hardback

ISBN-13: 978-0-7153-2286-4 paperback
ISBN-10: 0-7153-2286-9 paperback

Printed in China by SNP Leefung
for David & Charles
Brunel House   Newton Abbot   Devon

Executive Editor Cheryl Brown
Editor Jennifer Proverbs
Head of Design Prudence Rogers
Designer Jodie Lystor
Production Controller Ros Napper
Project Editor Juliet Bracken

Visit our website at www.davidandcharles.co.uk

David & Charles books are available from all good bookshops; alternatively you can
contact our Orderline on 0870 9908222 or write to us at FREEPOST EX2 110, D&C Direct,
Newton Abbot, TQ12 4ZZ (no stamp required UK only); US customers call 800-289-0963
and Canadian customers call 800-840-5220.

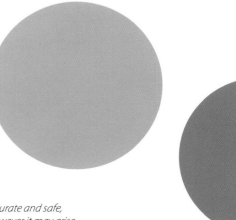

Contents

It's Play Time!

Everyone loves to receive a handmade card and children are no exception. If you already enjoy making cards, the good news is that you can be even more inventive when it comes to making cards for a child's special day — and your efforts are sure to be appreciated.

I hope the designs in this book will inspire you to create ingenious cards for children you know — whether they are your own or your friends' kids. I have catered for many different ages and occasions and included plenty of fun interactive ideas, such as flaps to lift, sliders to pull and tags to remove.

It can be tricky to get the tone right for a particular age group because children move on quickly to new tastes and interests. So I have included designs that will appeal at different stages in their lives, from when they are very young to the fashion-conscious older teens. There's a mini memory album that new parents will always treasure and a multi-pocket design

to celebrate a child's first day at school. There are ghostly Halloween cards that older children will love, and for those who have nearly reached adulthood and can be so hard to buy for, I have created some stylish ways to present a gift token.

Christmas and birthdays are the most popular occasions to make cards for, but there are lots of other milestones that call for a special handmade greeting too, such as a christening or naming day, and success in a sports contest, music or ballet exam. Children appreciate a card that celebrates their own interests.

I have tried above all to make each design a visual delight for a child to discover by using a selection of the exciting papers and embellishments you can buy. You will find yourself spoiled for choice when it comes to choosing these materials and there's a wealth of exciting papers, stickers, embellishments and charms to discover. You can convey lots of fun storylines through colours, texture and patterns. I also found the huge range of scrapbooking papers and stickers ideal for cardmaking.

I hope this book will be the starting point for you to create your own fun projects for the children you know. Once you start, you'll be amazed by what your imagination can come up with.

Card Games

Card and paper are the key elements in the card making process. There are hundreds of different types to choose from, many of which are ideal for creating original and imaginative cards for children.

Paper trail

You can buy both paper and card in a range of different weights. However, the weight is more important for card than paper because you are unlikely to use a paper on its own. If I find a nice paper I want to use as a background, I always stick it to thick card, as a solid base for a greetings card.

Colours of the rainbow

There are lots of gorgeous coloured papers you can buy. Use them to create the right mood or to tell a story on a card. For example, the cool grey and lilac of the papers used on the embellished card on page 44 made me think of a minimalist design that would appeal to a teenage boy.

Vital statistics

Card comes in various colours, weights and finishes. The weight is measured in grammes per square metre (gsm). Choose a 260gsm card if you need it to stand up without buckling, and a thinner card, for example 140gsm, for making cut-outs to stick to cards. This is also a good weight for templates, as you can draw round it easily and it is strong enough to be used frequently.

Clever finish

Pearlescent, metallic, glitter, holographic and iridescent papers reflect light in exciting ways, for example by changing colour. I made a mobile phone from silver holographic paper for the design on page 57.

Pretty patterns

One good way to add colour and pattern to cards is by using scrapbooking paper. There is a huge choice of different designs, from florals and optical effects to animal prints, camouflage and denim effect. You can use the paper as an all-over background, as on the wardrobe lift-the-flap card on page 50, or as highlights, as on the card for holding a music token on page 66.

Texture and pattern

Using papers with a fun texture, such as hammered, flock and corrugated, will enhance your cards and make them appeal to children. The stretch limo on page 37 has a pink background paper covered in sparkling silver dots.

Ready to use

You can use pre-cut, pre-folded cards known as blanks which come in specific sizes with envelopes. They often have a window known as an aperture cut in them, through which you can display photos, stickers and other embellishments. They work out more expensive, but are handy if you're in a hurry.

Child's Play

One sheet of paper goes a long way, so making a card is an ideal way of using up leftover pieces from a scrapbooking session.

Dressing Up

You can add some exciting finishing touches to cards for children using fun embellishments such as stickers, charms, ribbon and sequins. These are available from craft and hobby shops, by mail-order and online, and there are plenty to choose from.

Child's Play
Embellishments are popular with children, but small items should not be used on cards for very young children because they are a choking hazard.

Fun shapes

There are lots of fabulous, small, moulded embellishments that will add the perfect finishing touch to a card. These can either be suspended from chain and cord like the charms on a charm bracelet, or laid flat and glued directly to the card, as with the pencil case charms on the Starting School card on page 26.

Cool badges

You can spell out a message on a card using small round frames filled with card discs. These can be decorated with numbers, letters or stickers and are held in place by prongs folded flat on the back. They are ideal for children's cards because they look like badges and are used on the embellished birthday card on page 46.

Sensational stickers

Stickers are just what you need to decorate a plain background. They come in many different styles – for example, illustrated or photographic – and sizes. Scrapbooking suppliers are a good source for photo stickers. These tend to come in a large format for scrapbook pages, but there are plenty of images to choose from. You can also get word and message stickers for adding greetings to cards.

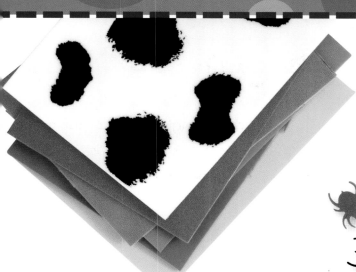

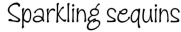

Sparkling sequins

Sequins are ideal for adding flashes of colour to cards. They come in many different shapes and are available from craft and sewing shops. The flowers are my favourites. You can also buy sequins without holes or confetti, from party shops. You can use this to fill shaker cards like the ones on pages 58 to 65, and you can buy confetti shapes for various celebrations.

Funky foam

You can make your own fun embellishments for children's cards using coloured foam, like I did for the journal cards on page 74. This foam is sold by the sheet, or in a huge range of pre-cut, colourful shapes. It is easy to cut with scissors or a craft knife and attach using PVA glue. You can also buy self-adhesive foam.

Stamp your mark

Stamps are perfect for adding motifs and highlights and there are now so many designs available that I could devote a whole book to them! Peel-off rubber stamps are one recent innovation that I find useful. These are attached to clear perspex blocks, allowing you to see through to the paper and avoid disappointing and time-consuming mistakes.

Basic Tool Kit

There are only a few basic tools and materials you need before you can make a start on the projects in this book. You will probably already have some of them in your home.

Craft knife

A craft knife is essential for cutting long straight lines. It is much neater and more accurate than a pair of scissors. It's also useful for cutting inside a shape where it would be difficult to insert the points of the scissors without creasing the paper. I use a scalpel with detachable, 10A cutting blades that are light and easy to hold, and allow for very precise cutting.

Child's Play
Remember to change the blades on a craft knife regularly.

Masking tape

I use a removable, low-tack masking tape to keep small pieces of paper or card in place while I work. It is also good for securing pieces while you draw around them.

Cutting mat

Always use a cutting mat with a craft knife to protect your work surface. These have a rubber, self-sealing surface that stays flat and smooth after use. They are marked with a gauge so you can line up card or paper and then cut a perfectly straight line every time. There are various sizes to choose from.

Compass

Use a compass to draw a circle of a specific diameter. Some compasses have a handy gauge so you can check your circle is accurate. Some also have a detatchable arm which allows you to draw an extra large circle.

Scissors

Craft scissors are ideal for cutting paper and card, foam, fabric and other materials. You may wish to have a small pair of sharp-pointed scissors as well. These are essential for snipping into inaccessible areas. You can also buy scissors that have different shaped blades, such as zigzag, wavy, scallop or turret. These are available singly or in sets. Metal blades tend to cut more precisely than plastic ones.

Rulers

Always use a metal ruler (ideally one with a slightly raised centre) when cutting with a craft knife, and keep fingers away from the blade. Use a plastic ruler for basic measuring and drawing straight lines on card and paper.

Pencil

Use a soft-leaded pencil (for example, B, 2B or 3B) for tracing patterns and marking measurements, as softer pencil marks are easier to rub out. Use a rubber or plastic eraser to rub out, but keep your eraser clean to prevent it marking the surface of your card.

Tracing paper

This translucent paper is used to transfer a pattern from a book or magazine on to card or another material (see page 17). It is sold as loose sheets or in a pad, and comes in various sizes.

Adhesives

There are many different adhesives to try. A glue stick is a clean and easy adhesive to use on paper and card. Use double-sided tape to stick paper to card and to attach non-porous items like plastic, embellishments and foam. PVA glue is also good for attaching embellishments to cards, but is too liquid for adding layers of paper onto card.

Eyelet kit

Eyelets are metal rivets used to join items together. They are inserted through a hole punched with an eyelet punch and hammered flat on the back with a setter tool (see page 16). Eyelets are used for decoration on cards as much as for practical purposes.

Single punch

A single paper punch is useful for punching precise holes, for example in the top of a tag, as you can see exactly where you are placing the hole.

Easy as 1, 2, 3

Card making is a straightforward hobby with few complicated techniques to learn. Once you have the basic materials to hand, you can get on with producing cards without much fuss. For a professional look, you need to pay some attention to detail. These guidelines will help you get it right.

Scoring and folding

Scoring your paper before it is folded creates a nice crisp fold and gives a more professional looking finish. It also makes the job of folding much easier.

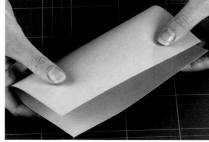

1 Make two pencil marks where you want the score line to go on the back of the card or paper. Line up a ruler with these marks and score very lightly down the edge using one blade from a pair of scissors or a craft knife.

2 Gently fold the card along the scored line using both hands. You should find it folds easily.

3 Press along the fold to make it sharp using a bone folder or the back of a clean metal spoon.

Child's Play

Alternatively, use a ruler to fold your paper (or card) neatly. Measure your paper to find the centre, then place your ruler against this line. Fold the paper over your ruler, using the edge as a guide. Whichever method you choose, you can be sure of neat folds every time.

Covering a card with paper

Covering a folded card neatly with paper can be tricky, but this method will produce professional results when you are using a printed scrapbooking paper as a background for a card. There won't be any unsightly peeling at the edges because the paper extends around the fold to the back of the card.

1 Cut some thick white card to size, score and fold it in half (see left). Cut your patterned paper 1cm larger than the card on three sides, and long enough to cover the card front and about a quarter of the back. Spread paper glue on the front of the card and press this down onto the back of the paper, leaving space all round to trim.

2 Lay the card front face down on a cutting mat and allow it to close. Trim away the excess paper from three sides of the card. Trim the overlap to about a quarter of the width of the card back.

3 Spread glue over the overlap on the back of the card and press the paper down on to it. Close the card and re-crease the fold.

Covering a tag

Decorated tags like the ones on page 92 make dynamic focal points and add an original touch to a card. It's fun and inexpensive to make your own tags rather than buying them ready-printed.

1 Take a plain white swing tag and remove the string. Spread paper glue over one side of the tag and press it down onto decorative paper or thin card. Leave to dry for about 10 minutes.

2 Carefully trim away the excess paper around the edges of the tag. For a really neat finish, trim around the curved section at the top of the tag with a craft knife.

3 Place the tag face down on a craft mat. Mark the position of the punched hole by pressing the card firmly with a ballpoint pen or pencil. Turn the tag over. Re-punch the tag where marked, using an eyelet setter (see page 16).

Applying glitter

Glitter is a fun material that children really love. It doesn't have to be reserved for Christmas and you can make glittering cards for many occasions from Hallowe'en to Easter! Glitter glue is suitable for adding sparkling highlights, but PVA glue with loose glitter is best for covering a large area.

1 Cut out the shape you want to cover from thick white card. Place on scrap paper and spread a thin layer of PVA glue over the surface.

2 Sprinkle a generous amount of glitter over the glue, making sure all of it is covered. Leave the glue to set for about 10 minutes.

3 Carefully pick up the shape and gently shake off the excess glitter. Lay the shape flat to dry. Pour the remaining glitter back into the container to use again.

Using eyelets

Eyelets come in various sizes, so you will need to insert the correct diameter head for your eyelets in the punch before you make any holes. The punch is put in position, then tapped smartly with a small hammer to cut a hole. An eyelet is inserted through the hole and the paper turned over. The back of the eyelet is hammered flat with the eyelet setter to keep it in place. Protect your work surface before using the eyelet tool.

1 Place the items to be attached on a cutting mat. Screw the correct diameter head onto the punch. Mark the position of the eyelet, then punch a hole at this point. Punch a matching hole in the second item.

2 Match the holes on each item and push an eyelet through both of them from front to back.

3 Place the cards face down on the cutting mat. Insert the pointed end of the setter into the back of the eyelet and hammer it to flatten it into a ring shape.

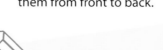

Child's Play
The punch comes with a series of detachable heads. Each one is a paper punch of a different diameter, allowing you to use different size eyelets.

Transferring a pattern

Unless you have a very good eye (or steady hand) you will need to transfer the patterns on pages 98 to 110 to make the cards in this book. You can either trace them on to thin card and cut them out as templates to draw round, or transfer the pattern directly onto your paper or card with tracing paper and a pencil.

1 Trace your chosen pattern from pages 98 to 109. Place the tracing face down onto thin white card and draw over the lines to transfer the pattern. Cut out the template and draw around it onto the paper or card of your choice.

2 To transfer a pattern straight on to paper or card, place your tracing face down and carefully draw over the lines again with a pencil. Remove the tracing and lightly draw over the lines again if they are a little faint.

3 If you don't feel confident about following the line of the pattern neatly, place the tracing face down and scribble over the lines to transfer them. You can then flip the tracing back the right way and redraw over the original lines to transfer the pattern.

Child's Play

You can also use transfer paper to copy a pattern onto paper or card. This has a coloured, waxy surface on one side. Put it face down on the paper with the tracing on top, then draw over the pencil lines. They will be reproduced perfectly. Whichever method you choose will result in an accurate pattern that can be used on one or several cards.

Concertina Keepsakes

Folded cards that open out to reveal a series of treasured items collected over time are a wonderful way to record an important milestone in a child's life. A simple concertina folding card can be used, for example, to chronicle a child's precious first year or to record a one-off event like their first day at school. Stamps, tags and embellishments will make the perfect alternative when you don't have many treasures you can use.

My First Year, opposite, is a mini album of mementos and photographs that makes a charming child's first birthday card. It will delight grandparents and godparents and keep them in touch with the important milestones. The main focus of the card is baby's photograph, displayed on a tag. Immediately inside is a first birthday cake sticker which links the basic elements of the card together. The concertina opens to reveal more mementoes, such as a little sock and a lock of hair.

A baby's first year flies by so quickly. Look back on this joyful time with a fold-out collection of precious memories, fronted by their smiling face.

My First Year

You will need:

✎ Thick white card, 17.5 x 14cm (7 x 5½in) ✎ Cream paper
✎ Luggage label ✎ Baby photos and mementoes
✎ Pink twine ✎ Self-adhesive ribbon
✎ Baby photos and mementoes
✎ Wavy-edge scissors

1

Fold the thick white card in half, and glue the rectangle of gingham paper to the card front (see page 15). Fold the excess to the back before gluing it in place.

2

Cut a piece of cream paper the same width as the luggage label and 4cm (1½in) shorter. Cut a decorative border along the top and bottom edges with zigzag-edge scissors. Glue the paper in the centre of the label.

3

Attach a length of paper ribbon sticker across the lower edge of the label and trim it to fit.

Pink gingham paper, 17.5 x 14cm (7 x 5½in) plus extra for decoration
 Paper ribbon sticker Five daisy stickers Heart-shaped button
 Zigzag-edge scissors Basic tool kit (see page 12)

Child's Play

Collect such treasures as buttons from favourite clothes, scraps of fabric and cherished pictures to build up a snapshot of significant milestones. Look out for themed baby stickers that will add the perfect finishing touches.

4

Use wavy-edge scissors to cut narrow borders from cream paper for the lower edge of the label and the top and bottom of the card. Cut a wavy gingham border for the top of the paper ribbon sticker. Glue them all in place.

5

Cut a 4.5cm (1¾in) square from gingham paper. Draw a 1cm (⅜in) smaller square in the centre and carefully cut this out with a craft knife to make a frame. Glue the frame to the label.

6

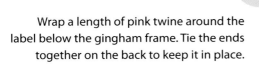

Wrap a length of pink twine around the label below the gingham frame. Tie the ends together on the back to keep it in place.

7

Remove the string from the top of the label. Stick a daisy sticker over the hole, then punch a hole through the sticker (see page 12) and tie a length of pink twine through it (see finished photograph). Glue a heart-shaped button in the centre of the paper ribbon sticker.

8

Glue your baby photo to thin card and trim it to fit inside the frame. Attach a foam pad in each corner on the back and glue the photo in the middle of the frame.

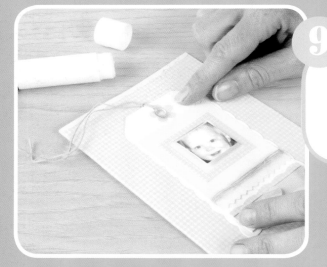

9

Glue the label to white card and trim around it with wavy edge scissors to give it a decorative border. Glue the mounted label to the card front.

10

Attach pink and yellow daisy stickers below the label. Arrange the ends of the pink twine and secure them with another daisy sticker in the top left corner of the card.

11

To make the concertina, cut three, 15.5 x 22cm (6 x 8¾in) pieces of cream paper. Glue them together, overlapping the edges by 1cm (½in) and leave to dry. Then fold into five equal sections (see page 14).

12

Child's Play

Mount small or fiddly items like a lock of hair on to a small tag or swing ticket first for a neater, more uniform appearance.

Glue a small memento, photo or sticker to each page of the concertina and decorate with a border of self-adhesive ribbon (see finished card below). Stick the concertina to the inside of the card as shown and fold up the pages.

More Concertina Fun!

On the road

Passing a driving test is an important rite of passage for a teenager that deserves a special card. I used an old map to make a fun background for my driving test success card.

The concertina card opens out to reveal a collection of little paper charms and symbols such as traffic lights and car keys. At the bottom of each page are some speed limit signs that accelerate from 0–50 across the card. You can buy old maps quite cheaply in car boot sales, junk shops and flea markets that will provide enough material for several cards. Cake decorating shops are an ideal source for good luck symbols such as horseshoes and clover leaves.

Birthday surprise

Children enjoy puzzles so this card has been designed as a series of clues to a surprise birthday treat. I used bold, contemporary scrapbook papers that will appeal to slightly older children.

On the front is a cropped photo sticker of a lion's head on a luggage label. Arrows lead the child inside the card, where more photo stickers have been trimmed to disguise the identities of various animals. I cut out the large question and exclamation marks from the same paper to continue the fun, quirky theme. The final sticker, showing the whole of the lion's head, reveals the answer is a trip to a safari park.

Pocketful of Memories

Here's a fun idea for a card – a visual diary or collection of mementos and keepsakes on a special theme. It's created by filling a sheet of the transparent pockets used for photographic slides with stickers, embellishments, photos and other precious items. The pockets are just the right size for showcasing such treasures and many different occasions can be celebrated in this charming way. You can also use this format to give a fresh twist to a traditional advent calendar.

Starting school is an important milestone that calls for a special card. Pocket cards are perfect for this age group, as young children love collections of small objects. What's more, this style of design can be open-ended. The child who receives the card can keep adding to it, for example when they receive a star or sticker for good work at school, or with photos of classmates. It will also make a lovely leaving card at the end of the summer term.

Create a fun visual diary celebrating a child's first day at school as a special keepsake they can look back on in years to come.

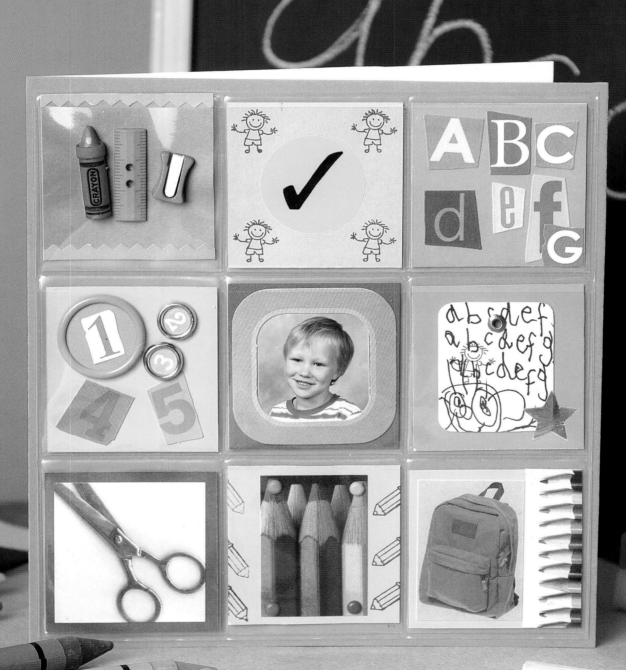

Starting School

You will need:

- Thick white card, 36 x 18cm (14 x 7in)
- Little boy stamp and red ink pad
- Clear 35mm slide pockets
- Pencil case charms
- Pencil stamp and blue ink pad
- Child's photo and card frame
- Paper fasteners

1 Cut out a square of nine pockets from the slide sheet. Trim away the excess plastic as close as possible to the seams for a neat finish.

2 Measure and cut out nine, 5.3cm (2in) squares of coloured paper to fit inside the pockets. Decorate them as explained in steps 3–8.

3 Apply a 'tick' sticker in the middle of the blue paper square, then stamp a little boy with red ink in each corner.

4 Stamp three sets of pencils down each side of the light blue square using blue ink. Add a crayons photo sticker in the centre. Punch a small hole in each corner of the sticker, and insert a paper fastener in each hole.

5 Attach a school bag photo sticker to the yellow square, positioning it off-centre. Trim another crayon sticker to leave only the pencil tops showing and stick it vertically down the side of the paper.

- Paper in a selection of colours ✎ Crayon, scissors, schoolbag, tick stickers
- Orange card dot and green frame ✎ Lilac number dots and silver frames
- Aqua, self-adhesive foam, 18cm (7in) square ✎ Basic tool kit (see page 12)

7

Push out the centre of the card frame. Glue the photo of the child to the back, then attach it to the red paper square.

6

Push out an orange card dot and insert it into a green frame. Decorate with a number 1 sticker. Insert a number 2 dot and a number 3 dot into two small silver frames. Glue them all to the lime green paper square, then add an unframed number 4 sticker and number 5 sticker as well.

8

Decorate one orange square with alphabet stickers. Attach three pencil case charms to a blue square before trimming the edges with wavy edge scissors and sticking this to another orange square.

9

Reduce a child's drawing in size on a photocopier, then trace it onto a tag and add lettering in the style of a child's handwriting. Stamp another little boy onto the tag and attach it to the final green square with a star eyelet (see page 16)

✎ Child's Play
To make the writing and drawing on the alphabet tag look as authentic as possible, do it with your left hand (or vice versa if you're left-handed).

10

Insert each decorated square carefully into a pocket, positioning the photo in the centre. Fold the thick white card in half and stick the foam to the front. Attach a small piece of double-sided tape to the back of each pocket, then mount the completed square onto the card, pressing it firmly into place.

More Mini Pocket Ideas

Naming day

Here's one of the nicest cards you can make: the invitation to your baby's christening. Slide pockets are ideal for this occasion because you can place little mementos, photos and stickers in each pocket, in effect making several cards in one.

I put baby's photo in the first pocket, wrote her date of birth on a tag and trimmed this with punched silver hearts and buttons for the second pocket. The third pocket features a little christening gown cut from white paper and trimmed with ribbon and two pearly flower sequins. In the final pocket is a beautiful photo sticker and three little punched duck shapes. I used a dotted lilac scrapbooking paper for the background.

Eggcellent fun

This card is designed as an Easter egg hunt. Each pocket contains a little card made from folded pieces of scrapbooking paper decorated with either egg shapes cut from more paper or Easter eggs stamps.

Inside some of the cards are more Easter egg shapes embellished with stickers. The idea is for children to search for the eggs and receive a treat for each one they find. Alternatively, little chocolate bunnies could be hidden in some of the pockets. You will find a template for the egg on page 99.

Girlfriends forever

This card celebrates friendship, an important theme in a teenage girl's life. The top left pocket contains, naturally, a photo booth picture of two best friends.

The remaining pockets all have a background cut from funky scrapbooking paper. These can be decorated with poems, messages, drawings, or as here, with gorgeous embellishments. These are just some of the many add-ons you can buy that are aimed at teenage girls. Who could resist a tiny handbag and mobile phone, or a perfect little pair of shoes with holographic silver flower trim?

Countdown to Christmas

The start of advent is a special time for children when they are allowed to be excited about Christmas. Here is a mini advent calendar to celebrate the week running up to Christmas.

Each pocket is filled with a square of festive scrapbooking paper, some with a gingerbread house sticker on top. The other squares have a white tag decorated with a date added in gold rub-on numbers. These are attached with eyelets so they can move freely. To finish off, small plastic embellishments in festive colours were slipped inside the pockets. You could also add a chocolate treat beneath each date tag.

Watch Them Move

Adding movement to your cards is fun and easy using simple devices such as sliders and rotators. A slider bar sits inside a pair of slots and can be positioned at the back or front of a card; the moving object or figure is attached to the bar and pushed from side to side, or up and down. A rotator is attached with a paper fastener, which allows the object or figure to move in a circle like the rocket on page 67. These simple devices can be easily adapted to suit a particular design.

My Skateboard Sliders design uses the simplest moving device, a slider bar, to capture the spirit of this sport in a simple design that will appeal to an older age group. A brick-patterned dolls' house paper was used to create an urban-style background with a strip of green flock paper for the grass. The slider is on the front of the card and is disguised by making it the same colour and width as the ramp behind.

The slider bar moves smoothly through the slots of the card, giving the impression that the skateboarder is whizzing past — whoosh!

Skateboard Sliders

You will need:

✎ Thick white card, 20 x 30cm (8 x 12in)   ✎ Grey paper
✎ Green flock dolls' house paper, 1.5 x 20cm (½ x 8in)

1 Fold the white card in half. Glue the brick-patterned paper to the front. Fold the excess to the back and glue in place (see page 15).

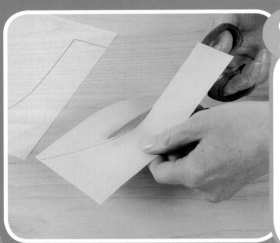

2 Trace the slope template from page 108. Flip the tracing and transfer the image to grey paper by drawing the lines again (see page 17). Cut out the slope.

3 Glue the slope to the front of the card, matching up the lower edges of each piece exactly.

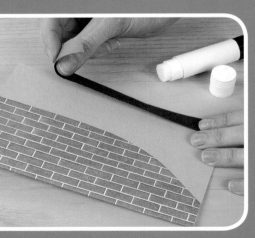

4 Glue the green flock paper in place along the card's lower edge.

5 Trace the slider template from page 108. Flip the tracing, then transfer the design to thin white card by drawing over the lines again. Cut out the slider, then glue it to grey paper and cut out.

🖊 Brick-patterned dolls' house paper, 20 x 15cm (8 x 6in)
🖊 Skateboard stickers 🖊 Basic tool kit (see page 12)

Child's Play

When you mark out the slots for a slider bar, make each one about 2mm (¹⁄₁₆in) longer than the width of the slider bar. This will enable the bar to move freely without buckling.

6 Using a craft knife and ruler over a cutting mat, cut two vertical slots in the grey slope near the left edge to hold the slider. Make them 1cm (³⁄₈in) apart and slightly longer than the width of the bar, and position them just above the green flock paper.

7 Insert the slider bar into the slots, cutting them slightly wider if necessary. The bar should fit snugly and move smoothly from side to side.

8 Stick the skateboarder sticker to the end of the slider, trimming off the excess card showing behind the sticker.

9 Add the other skateboarder stickers in the right places on the slope and the background wall.

More Moving Cards!

Peekaboo

Very young children will love sliding apart the present on this birthday card to reveal a cute gingham duck sticker. This element of surprise makes it the perfect design for babies who will enjoy looking for the duck again and again.

The construction of the card is very simple. Each half of the parcel is a folded piece of paper. The top half is attached to the slider which moves through slots cut in the lower half. The nursery-style wrapping paper was created by gluing on small polka dots punched from gingham paper. The ribbons are strips of paper cut with wavy-edged scissors and a button sticker was added over the join. A matching gift tag completes the card.

Child's Play

When making a rotating card, cover the legs of the split pins on the back of the card so that little fingers can't get at them. Use extra sticky sellotape, or cut a small square of paper and glue it in place.

Blast off!

This cosmic card made from shiny holographic paper will appeal to budding astronomers and astronauts. Blue paper printed with stars gives the effect of a twinkling night sky.

The stars and planets are made from stickers, and circles punched from silver and gold paper. The rocket is constructed with a bar glued vertically to the lower fin and attached to the centre of the card with a paper fastener. The fastener was loosely folded back on the reverse to allow the rocket to rotate freely across the top of the card. The fastener is covered with a square of paper on the back for safety. On the front a round moon made from holographic paper hides the bar and fastener.

Pa-a-a-r-rty night

This stretch limo design will make the perfect card for an eighteenth birthday. The end of the car slides back through a slot cut in the card to reveal the girls on a special night out.

The pink background paper covered in swirling silver dots adds a touch of glamour, while the car details created from delicate handmade and metallic papers add layers of luxury. Bright floral stickers add an essential dash of girly fun, and some stickers of trendy teenage girls complete the design.

Joggle-Eye Fun

You can make lots of fun cards using joggle eyes that will appeal to children of different ages. The eyes come in several sizes: generally, the large ones have most impact for small children, while the smaller ones are suitable for more grown up designs. Glitter, plastic jewels and shiny stickers can all be used to give cards a bold, three-dimensional feel and a vivid background will show off the shape of a design clearly.

The main design for this chapter, Easter Bunny, was made with medium-sized joggle eyes. The bunny's head is cut from bright white card and has shocking pink ears and hair detail, added with glitter glue. Glitter glue can be used both to cover large areas and apply fine lines, as here for the bunny's nose and mouth. Glitter glue has a high sheen and dries flat, so as a contrast, the bunny's cheeks were covered with silver glitter which is more textured and catches the light well.

Children will love this delightful Easter bunny. Listen out for their giggles when they shake the card and see the fun joggling eyes!

Easter Bunny

You will need:

✎ Thick pink card, 25 x 18cm (10 x 7in)
✎ 15mm (1/8in) wide pink organza ribbon ✎ Medium joggle eyes ✎ Silver glitter

1 Trace the rabbit template from page 106. Flip the tracing and transfer the image to thin card by drawing over the lines again (see page 17).

2 Carefully cut round the rabbit head, cutting just inside the pencil line.

3 Spread a thin coating of paper glue on the rabbit's cheeks. Sprinkle a thick coating of silver glitter over the glue, covering the pencil lines as well. Press your finger lightly over the glitter to make sure it adheres to the whole area.

Child's Play
Pour any excess glitter from the surface of the card back into the pot to use next time.

4 Draw over the rabbit's mouth with a thin line of pink glitter glue. Fill in the rabbit's hair and ears with a thin layer of the glue. Leave to dry thoroughly.

Thin white card, 20 x 14cm (8 x 5½in)
Pink glitter glue Basic tool kit (see page 12)

Child's Play

Avoid using the largest joggle eyes on small designs because they might look unbalanced or even scary.

5

Squeeze a dot of PVA glue onto the back of each joggle eye and attach them to the rabbit's face.

6

Cut a piece of thick pink card and fold it in half.

7

Glue the rabbit's head to the front of the card, lining up the lower edge of the rabbit's neck with the bottom of the card.

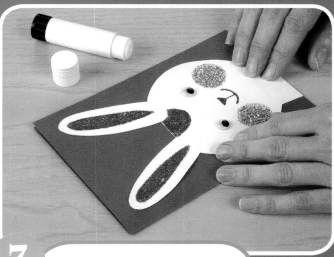

8

Cut a length of pink organza ribbon and tie it in a bow. Attach the bow to the middle of the rabbit's neck with a small dot of PVA glue.

More Pairs of Eyes

Hippy chick

This girl in a funky floral hat will appeal to youngsters who love clothes. One fun aspect of this design is that you can change the hair or other elements to match the recipient.

I used large daisy stickers to decorate the hat and smaller stickers, left over from the same sheet, to make the girl's necklace and highlight her cheeks – they were much too nice to waste. You can substitute other stickers you know would be popular.

The cat's whiskers

This friendly pussy cat will make the perfect birthday card for small children. The pipe cleaner whiskers and large joggle eyes make it especially appealing.

The soft and pretty face, ears and collar are cut from scraps of pastel coloured felt and the collar decorated with glued-on plastic gems. The design could be adapted for a slightly older age group by using stronger, more vibrant colours.

Vampire greetings

Here joggle eyes and a vivid orange background make this dramatic Hallowe'en card seem almost three-dimensional.

Count Dracula's head was cut from a ghostly shade of green card. His hair, true to vampire style, is cut from black paper and highlighted with a layer of dense black glitter. His eyes are attached with pink glitter glue, and sharp white fangs add the final, ghoulish touch. The bright orange background card gives a traditional hallowe'en feel.

Friendly Rudolf

Large joggle eyes are perfect for a bold design like this one of smiling Rudolf which will make a very appealing Christmas card.

The reindeer's head is cut from brown paper, and has silver glitter antlers, ears and facial features. Extending Rudolf's ears over the sides and his red chenille pom-pom nose, give the card a three-dimensional feel that small children will love. A large scale design like this can comfortably accommodate the biggest joggle eyes.

Child's Play
See pages 98–99 for the templates to make these joggle-eye cards.

Embellished with Style

Adding three-dimensional embellishments to cards gives a unique, handmade feel. I have used some of the lovely charms, sequins and other embellishments you can buy on the cards in this chapter. Many of these can be suspended from a chain or ribbon, and used to show a necklace or other piece of jewellery. The cards all follow the same basic format: they have a simple coloured border down the left hand side and the main focal point on the right.

It can be hard to get the tone right on a card for a teenage boy using just the right mix of colours and add-ons. The main focus on Cool Dude, opposite, is a tee-shirt cut from a purple camouflage-patterned paper with a length of silver beaded chain cord around the neck. From the chain hang little dog tags cut from thin silver card that have rounded corners and a small hole in the top of each one. I edged the purple border with star-shaped brads and spelled out the child's age with number dots.

The cool modern colours and bold, strong shapes used here should give this card plenty of appeal for a teenage boy.

Cool Dude

You will need:

✎ Thick white card, 29 x 14.5cm (11½ x 6¼in)
✎ Purple camouflage scrapbooking paper, one sheet
✎ Green circle tag ✎ Star brads, seven ✎ Eyelet punch and hammer

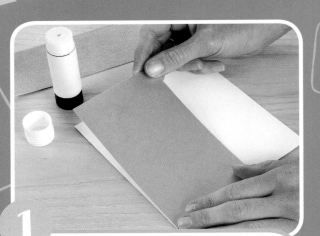

1 Fold the thick white card in half. Glue the silver paper to the right hand side of the card front and the purple paper to the left, butting up the edges on both pieces.

2 Trace the tee-shirt template from the pattern on page 99. Transfer the tracing to the purple camouflage paper (see page 17) and cut it out. Glue a semi-circle of purple paper to the top of the tee-shirt to make the neckline.

3 Glue the tee-shirt about 3cm (1¼in) down from the top on the silver area of the card.

Child's Play
You will find a pair of sharp-pointed craft or embroidery scissors helpful for rounding off the corners of the tags. They cut more precisely than general craft scissors.

4 To make the tags, cut two, 2 x 1cm (¾ x ⅜ in) rectangles of silver card. Cut off each corner on both pieces to round the edges, then punch a hole in the top of each one with the eyelet punch (see page 16).

✎ Silver paper, 9 x 14.5cm (3½ x 5¾in) ✎ Purple paper, 5.5 x 14.5cm (2¼ x 6¼in)
✎ Silver beaded cord, 10cm (4in) ✎ Purple number dots ✎ Silver dot holders
✎ Basic tool kit (see page 12)

Child's Play
Use a small glue dot rather than liquid glue to attach the numbers dots. It will give a much neater finish.

5 Punch two holes just above the neck of the tee-shirt. Thread the tags onto the length of beaded cord. Push the ends of the cord through the holes, trim, and tape them together on the back of the card to secure them.

6 Insert the number dots into the silver holders and push in the pins to secure them (see page 10).

7 Push the green circular tag out of the backing card and glue it to the silver card below the tee-shirt. Glue the number dots in the middle of the circle.

8 Cut a small slit in the purple border with a craft knife for each star brad. Position the first one 1cm (⅜in) down from the top and 1cm (⅜in) away from the edge of the silver border; space them 2cm (¾in) apart. Push the legs of a star brad through each slit and cover them with tape on the back.

More Ways to Embellish

Ghoulish greeting

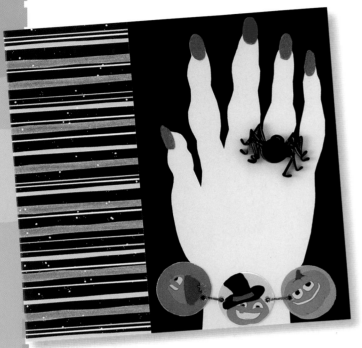

This ghoulish, girl's Halloween card features a bony witch's hand sporting a bracelet with charms made from pumpkin stickers attached to discs of coloured card.

The charms are threaded together with lurex cord that passes through punched holes around the witch's wrist. The hand is cut from pale green paper for an extra spooky feel using the template on page 100, and a plastic spider charm sits menacingly over one gnarled finger. The hand is mounted on black paper for maximum impact, and has a talon made from red paper on each finger. A panel made from striped scrapbooking paper continues the Halloween theme.

Rhinestone rock

These funky jeans are created using a denim sticker.

There was only enough denim to make the top of the jeans (see page 100 for the template), so I used pale blue, sparkly paper for the pockets and to fill in the rest of the legs. I decorated these with stick-on rhinestones and tiny confetti stars. The rhinestones come arranged in heart and flower patterns and you could transfer an entire motif if desired. Around the waist is a pale blue belt made from elastic, from which hangs a large, silver heart charm. The border is embellished with subtle, translucent vellum heart

Icy charms

I kept the design of this Christmas tree card as simple as possible to allow the star charm to become its focal point.

The charm is tied on with narrow, lilac ribbon, adding to the icy, slightly ethereal feel of the design. I used a blue dotted scrapbooking paper for the background that suggests a snowscene, filled the border with mother-of-pearl, flower sequins and added a satin ribbon edge. Small silver or mother-of-pearl sequins would also look good. Turn to page 108 for the tree template.

Fairy magic

This dainty fairy card will delight any little girl.

The fairy is easy to make from pretty, pastel papers and has a layered tutu of lace-effect paper (you will find the template on page 100). This is an ideal design for using up leftover scraps of paper and embellishments. It's fun to browse through old stickers and pots of sequins to find just what you need for that extra sparkle. Around the fairy's neck is a small wire and fabric butterfly – though not strictly a charm, it does make a lovely, and magical, necklace.

Lift the Flaps

Lift-the-flap cards are an absolute delight to children of all ages. They are very simple to make, and even the most basic paper engineering can look impressive. These cards vary enormously in design, and illustrate how easy it is to adapt the techniques. You can hide many different things under the flaps, such as stickers and stamped images or three-dimensional items, if you use craft pads to make a space for them between the layers.

The main card, What to Wear, will delight fashion-conscious girls. It has little doors and a drawer that open to reveal a tee-shirt and handbag. Each door has a daisy door handle kept in place by a metal eyelet and a mirror on the back made from silver mirror card. The card background, a fresh, contemporary scrapbooking paper, is an important part of the design. As a finishing touch, the front of the wardrobe is decorated with delicate stamped daisies.

Open the doors to this gorgeous mini wardrobe and you will discover a fashionable outfit waiting to be put on.

What to Wear

You will need:

- Thick white card, 19 x 28cm (7½ x 11in)
- Brown polka dot scrapbooking paper, 5.5 x 14cm (2¼ x 5½in)
- Daisy stamp
- Red ink pad
- Coat hanger embellishment

1 Fold the white card in half. Glue the green polka dot paper to the front. Fold the excess paper to the back of the card and glue in place (see page 15).

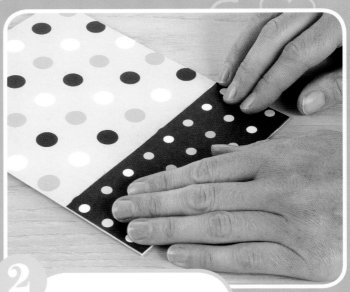

2 Glue the rectangle of brown polka dot paper to the card front, lining it up with the bottom of the card.

3 Trace the wardrobe and heart templates from page 101. Transfer the wardrobe to pink card and the heart to red paper (see page 17). Cut both out and glue the heart to the top of the wardrobe.

- Green polka dot scrapbooking paper, 19 x 16cm (7¼ x 6½in)
- Handbag pattern scrapbooking paper ✎ Thick pink card ✎ Red paper ✎ Mirror card
- Daisy punch ✎ Pink metallic eyelets and eyelet punch ✎ Craft pads ✎ Basic tool

Child's Play

Lightly score along the hinge of the doors and drawer to enable the flaps to open easily (see page 14).

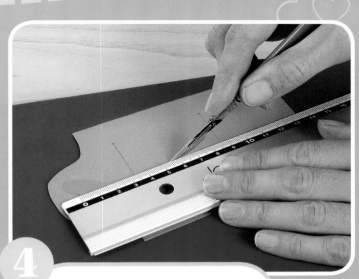

4 Place the wardrobe on a cutting mat. Use a metal ruler and a craft knife (see page 12) to cut open the flaps where marked on the pattern.

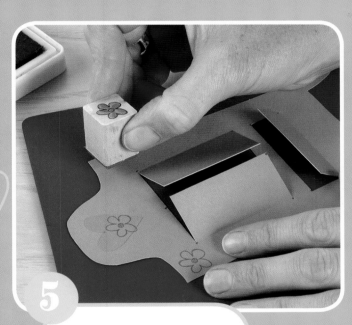

5 Stamp a daisy in the two top corners of the wardrobe. Then stamp one on the heart, and three along the lower edge.

6 Punch out three daisies from orange paper. Attach a daisy to each door and to the drawer front with an eyelet (see page 16), to make door knobs.

7

Cut two, 5 x 2cm (2 x ¾in) rectangles of mirror card. Glue one to the back of each door to look like a mirror.

8

Trace the tee-shirt template from page 101. Transfer the template to green dotted paper (see page 17) and cut out the tee-shirt.

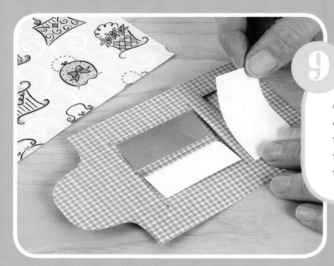

9

Cut a piece of handbag paper and glue it face down to the back of the wardrobe, covering the opening of the lower flap. Only apply glue to the very edges of the paper or it will stick to the back of the flap.

Child's Play

Make sure you raise the wardrobe sufficiently off the base card with craft pads for the doors to close over the coat hanger and tee-shirt.

10

Cut a piece of pink paper to form the back of the wardrobe and stick on with craft pads. Apply more craft pads to the top and bottom corners of the wardrobe.

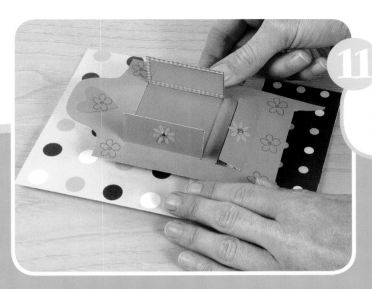

11 Place the wardrobe centrally on the card and press the corners gently to attach it to the background.

12 Glue the tee-shirt to the coat hanger. Open the wardrobe doors and glue the coat hanger to the pink paper inside the flaps. Leave open to dry.

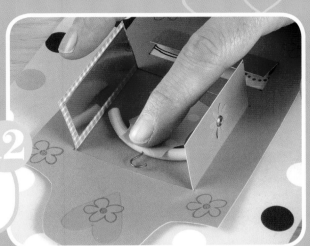

13 Once the glue has dried, carefully close both sets of flaps, ready for the card to be sent.

More Flaps to Lift

All tied up

I added an extra twist to the flaps on this card for a boy's birthday by tying them shut with string threaded through eyelets.

When untied the flaps fall down to reveal stickers underneath. The flaps are made from thin card covered with either a camouflage pattern scrapbooking paper or a denim sticker. Each flap is decorated with a numbered disc mounted in a mini frame. You could add a child's name or age, or a short message instead. I used skateboard stickers, but you could choose others that better reflect your child's interests and hobbies.

All I want for Christmas...

Here's a quick and simple lift-the-flap design that makes an eyecatching festive greeting.

I cut out the tree pattern on page 103 four times from green paper, trimmed a different amount from three of them so that they overlap when glued on top of each other. I mounted them on a sparkling red background, and added baubles punched from scraps of foil paper in seasonal colours. To accentuate the simplicity of the design, I cut a band of white paper with zigzag scissors and glued it below the tree to make snow. Under the flaps are hidden present stickers.

Up beat

Many children learn a musical instrument at school, and I designed this card to celebrate the hard work that goes into passing music exams or playing in the orchestra.

I chose a subtle scrapbooking paper design with wavy lines that resemble a musical score for my background. I added a large treble clef at the side of the card (see page 100 for a template), then made some stylized notes from circles of toning paper with staves that match the treble clef. The circles are lightly scored and lift up to reveal various musical stickers.

C U L8R

Mobile phones have achieved iconic status amongst teenagers, for whom only the smallest, most technologically advanced model will do.

I had fun making a replica of the latest photo phone, complete with flip top and tiny camera. The phone is cut from patterned, holographic paper (see page 101 for the templates). The top lifts up to reveal a stamped 'photo' of a girl smiling and number pads made from brightly coloured, 3D smiley stickers. I coloured the stamp in with pencil crayons and stuck the phone to a card covered with a striped scrapbooking paper in bright, sugary colours.

Shake It Up

Shaker cards are fun and lively, and especially appealing to children. The basic design incorporates an acetate-fronted box filled with small loose items which move around when the card is shaken. Glitter, beads, buttons and metallic confetti are all suitable; you could use sand and shells to celebrate a holiday or pretty cake candles for a birthday. The acetate window usually has a scene or character on its back wall. Stickers, cut-outs and funky foam shapes are good for decorating the insides of a shaker.

This jolly snowman stands inside the winter wonderland of a festive paper cracker. His body is stencilled with snow-effect paint which is heavily textured and dries to a convincingly snowy finish. Marker pens create his features and the hat, scarf and buttons are punched from scraps of paper. Punched paper snowflakes in two shades of blue flutter past him when the card is shaken, and the cracker is completed with rows of paper dots and bright stripes.

Who can resist shaking up this fun card to watch the snowflakes gather around the snowman?

Jolly Snowman

You will need:
✎ Thick white card, 16 x 21cm (6¼ x 8¼in)
✎ Lime green dotted scrapbooking paper, one sheet ✎ Black paper
✎ Clear acetate, small piece ✎ Stencil card ✎ Snow-effect paint

1 Fold the rectangle of white card in half lengthways. Glue the green paper to the front, then fold the excess to the back of the card and glue in place (see page 15).

2 Trace the cracker template on page 102. Place the tracing face down on the holographic paper and draw over the lines again to transfer the image (see page 17). Cut out the cracker, remove the backing from the paper, and stick it to the front of the card.

3 Cut two, 15mm (½in) wide strips of lime green dotted paper. Cut the edges with zigzag scissors and glue to either end of the cracker as decorative bands.

Green paper, 10 x 21 cm (4 x 8¼in) Self-adhesive silver holographic paper, one sheet
 Paper, light blue, dark blue, more colours Lime green self-adhesive foam, small piece
 Snowflake punch Red and black marker pens Basic tool kit (see page 12)

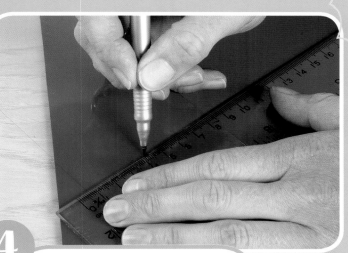

4 Trim the acetate to measure 7 x 8cm (2¾in x 3⅛in). Cut another piece of lime green dotted paper the same size.

5 Trace the snowman template on page 102. Place it face down on the stencil card and draw over the lines again to transfer the image. Cut out the snowman using a craft knife and cutting mat (see page 12).

6 Place the stencil centrally on the lime green dotted paper and dab snow-effect paint over the cut out section with a sponge to stencil the design onto the paper.

 Child's Play

You may have to apply two or three coats of snow-effect paint to get the desired depth of colour. Allow each coat to dry thoroughly before applying the next one to avoid overloading the card with moisture.

7

When the snowman is dry, draw his eyes, nose, mouth and cheeks with a marker pen. Punch two circles from black paper for buttons and cut out a small black hat. Glue them in place. Glue the snowman paper in the centre of the cracker.

Child's Play

Use a waterproof marker pen to apply the snowman's features. The ink from non-waterproof pens tends to bleed which can make the lines blurred.

8

Cut four, 5mm (⅛in) wide strips of lime green self-adhesive foam. Attach around the edges of the green dotted paper and trim to fit.

9

Punch five snowflakes from the light blue paper and five snowflakes from the dark blue paper. Place them over the snowman.

10

Attach thin strips of double-sided tape around the edge of the underside of the acetate, peel off the backing and stick it to the foam strips.

11

Cut a 7 x 8cm (2¾ x 3⅛in) piece of red paper. Draw and cut out a 6cm (2⅜in) circle in the middle of it.

12

Glue the red paper over the shaker box to make a frame.

Child's Play

Check that the shaker box and frame are well stuck down to ensure no shaker pieces escape – these can be a choking hazard for small children.

13

Cut two thin strips of blue paper and glue them across the top of the green dotted band at each end of the cracker. Punch 10 coloured dots and glue five to each dotted band. Glue two thin green strips across the top and bottom of the red paper.

More Shaker Surprises

Shimmering Swan Lake

This pretty birthday card will delight a budding ballerina. I made a little theatre using striped scrapbooking paper for the stage.

The dancers are stickers attached to the back of the shaker box. When the card is shaken tiny silver stars cascade down over them. It is crucial to the finished effect to use stars on the right scale: they should be as dainty as possible or they may overshadow the stickers. The tactile lilac 'curtains' that surround the stage (see page 102 for the template) are trimmed with thin gold ribbon and little gold bows for tie-backs.

Halloween horrors

The shaker on this scary card contains a leering skull cut from silver holographic paper. As this paper is iridescent, it changes colour and appearance when shaken, giving an exciting 3D effect.

The shaker is filled with orange, black and white halloween confetti in the shape of spiders. These slide creepily over the skull (see page 102 for the template) and drop to the bottom of the shaker in a suitably sinister way. The shaker box has a frame of dense black glitter and the card background is covered with a spidery scrapbooking paper.

Snow dome shaker

Snow domes are irresistible to all age groups – I should know, I've been collecting them for years. Although it doesn't have to be connected with Christmas, the basic design of a snow dome is perfect for the yuletide season.

I couldn't resist using it to make a Christmas shaker card. All the elements in the design are cut from coloured foam. The shaker is a snow dome containing a Christmas stocking. Silver glitter cascades over the stocking when the card is shaken and gold stars twinkle all around on a seasonal, red background.

Key to the door

This design makes a stylish coming of age card for girls. I chose aqua and mocha background papers to create an elegant look reminiscent of dress fabrics.

The bands of colour are edged with narrow satin ribbon and the shaker box is created from a little silver frame. I backed the frame with contrasting paper and filled it with metallic, star and 18 confetti shapes. The frame was finished off with a narrow, organza ribbon bow and attached to the background with double-sided tape.

Child's Play

Small photo frames make ideal shakers. They must be deep enough to hold the confetti and large enough for the contents to move when the card is shaken.

Token of Appreciation

I hope these cards will inspire you to transform a simple gift token into a fun surprise for a child's birthday or other occasion. They are designed to match the theme of a particular gift token, for example, a music token is attached to a mirror card CD, and a baby token slots into a towelling nappy. They will also give you the perfect excuse to go mad with embellishments. Add whatever you find that fits the theme, but remember to leave enough space for the token!

Bag a Bargain, opposite, is designed to hold a music token attached to an actual size, mirror card CD. The CD slots comfortably into a square format envelope transformed into a groovy bag for music-loving teenage girls. I used vibrant, clashing colours and a retro-style stamp to give my bag a young, fun look. I cut an edging and handle from spotted scrapbooking paper and tied on a matching decorated tag. The envelope has a button and string fastening.

Opening this stylish envelope bag to find the music token it conceals will make a wonderful birthday surprise.

Bag a Bargain

You will need:

✎ Thick white card, A4 sheet ✎ Mirror card, 15cm (6in) square
✎ Lime green dotted scrapbooking paper, one sheet
✎ Heart punch ✎ Pink metallic eyelets ✎ Small coin and CD

1

Lay one of the pink envelopes face down and stamp the flower design onto the flap. Leave to dry for a few minutes.

2

Stamp the design onto the lime green dotted paper. Place a small coin over the two daisy designs, then draw around them to make two circles. Cut out the circles.

3

Carefully open out the envelope, and lay it flat. On the right side of the envelope, attach the daisy circles to the top and bottom flaps with eyelets (see page 16). Glue the envelope back together again.

- Thin silver card, small piece - Two pink envelopes, 14cm (5½in) square
- Blue dotted scrapbooking paper, one sheet - Flower stamp - Red ink pad
- Wavy edge scissors - Pink lurex cord - Sticky dots - Basic Tool Kit (see page 12)

Cut five, 1cm (⅜in) strips of lime green dotted paper to decorate the envelope. Cut a wavy edge on three of the strips. Glue two wavy strips to the underside of the flap so that the decorative edge shows on the front, the third wavy strip across the bottom, and the other two strips down the sides as shown.

Child's Play
You can use any of the decorative edge scissors; you don't have to stick to wavy edge ones.

Trace the tag template from page 103. Stamp the front of the second pink envelope with the flower design. Transfer the tag pattern to the stamped paper (see page 17) and cut it out. Decorate the three longer sides with more strips of green dotted paper trimmed with wavy edge scissors.

Punch two hearts from the thin silver card. Punch a hole in one and attach it to the top of the tag with an eyelet (see page 16).

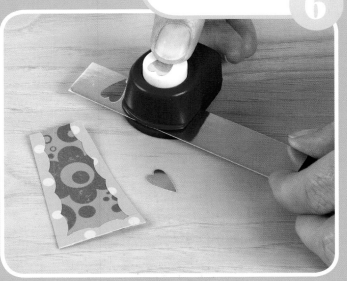

7

Punch two daisies from the lime green dotted paper. Glue them in the centre of the red stamped flowers, one on the envelope flap and one on the tag.

8

Cut a 1cm (⅜in) wide, 30cm (12in) long strip of lime green dotted paper and fold it diagonally in two places to make a handle shape. Glue this to the back of the envelope bag.

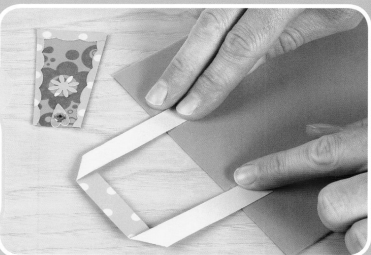

9

Fold the sheet of white card in half and cover the front with blue dotted paper (see page 15). Glue the envelope bag to the card, leaving the handle free.

10

Draw around a CD on the mirror card and cut out the circle. Draw a smaller circle with a compass on the second pink envelope, cut it out and stick it to the silver card. Add a sticky dot in the centre. Attach your token to the back of this card CD and push it into the envelope.

11

Cut a length of pink lurex cord and tie it to the tag through the eyelet hole. Then tie the tag to handle of the envelope bag.

12

Punch a hole in the second silver heart. Wrap a length of lurex cord around the two daisy circles to close the bag, and tie on the heart.

More Fun Gift Solutions

Ghost story

Knowing how much children love fantasy and ghost stories, I chose a spooky theme for this card to hold a book token.

The grainy orange background paper on this card gives the impression of an ethereal glow. The house is cut from a charcoal grey scrapbooking paper and has irregular-shaped windows and a door, cut from orange and lime green paper. A wide slit was cut in the house along the roof line before it was stuck to the card. The book token is attached to a ghost cut from thin white card using the template on page 103. The ghost goes in the slit and can be pulled up and down in a spooky way to reveal the gift.

Retail therapy

Teenage girls love clothes but it can be safer to give them a birthday token rather than choose clothes for them. This card is designed to hold a clothes token and some birthday messages.

The pocket is a large sticker mounted on card to remove the stickiness and attached to a fresh, green gingham background with thin double-sided tape. Snap fasteners hold the top corners firmly in place so the clothes token can be slipped inside. Each of the three tags covered in scrapbooking paper on a clothes theme has a message written on the back. They were tucked into the pockets and pinned to the card with tiny pastel safety pins.

Accessorize

These cute pastel-coloured, vellum mini envelopes were perfect for decorating with stickers, sequins, and scraps of ribbon to transform them into a trio of dinky bags.

I created a fun background on the ivory card with vellum dots in three different sizes. I attached a vellum heart sticker to the flap of each envelope and glued a mother-of-pearl flower sequin on top. I added a length of self-adhesive satin ribbon across the lower edge of each envelope and glued a loop of pretty ribbon to the back for a handle. The bags are glued face down on the card, ready to be filled with little gifts.

Precious gift

The birth of a baby is a joyful occasion and this card will make a fun way to present a gift token to proud new parents.

It has a nappy made from a triangle of short-pile towelling cut from a baby's facecloth, that was folded into shape and held together at the points with a safety pin. This left a flap into which the token can be tucked. The background card is covered with lilac, pearlescent paper and has bands of matching gingham ribbon glued at the top and bottom. Little hearts punched from pink, lilac and blue paper are glued along the top band and pretty stickers added in two opposite corners.

Funky Foam Journals

Coloured foam is a fun, versatile material you can use to create unusual card designs. It is easy to cut and glue, especially if you choose a self-adhesive type. Here I used the foam to make the covers for a personal organizer-style journal as well as the embellishments for it. Each journal has a flap that opens to reveal a traditional card. As a further twist, there's a little booklet made from folded paper stuck to the back of the card for children to write in or draw on.

The main design for this chapter, Funky Garden, has a bright and colourful butterfly on its cover. This is created from layers of foam pieces and has a real three-dimensional feel. The tips of its antennae and its wings are finished with plastic jewels. Around the butterfly are scattered fat daisies with fabulous fake gem centres. The flap is held in place with a Velcro dot, and is hidden by a large orange daisy.

Children will love filling the blank pages of their foam journal with their own drawings and stories.

Funky Garden
You will need:

✎ Thick white card, 15.5 x 23cm (6¼in x 9in) ✎ Thin white card ✎ Self-adhesive foam, turquoise, pink, orange and red pieces

Child's Play
Coloured foam marks easily, so should be handled with care. Cut smooth edges on your template and when cutting it with scissors, take small snips into the foam rather than making a long cut.

1 Trace the journal cover from the templates on page 103. Transfer the tracing onto thin white card (see page 17) and cut it out to make a template.

2 Place the template on a sheet of foam and draw lightly around it, with a ballpoint pen rather than a pencil to prevent tearing. Cut the straight lines with a craft knife and ruler on a craft mat. Cut around the flap with small pointed scissors.

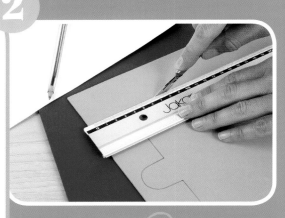

3 Transfer the flower and butterfly motifs on page 104 on to thin card (see page 17) and cut out to make templates. Draw around the flower onto turquoise, pink and orange foam. Draw around the butterfly's wings onto red foam and its body onto orange foam. Cut out all the pieces.

4 Fold the journal cover in half and crease the spine so you can visualize the amount of space available for the cut-outs. Lay the cover flat. Remove the paper backing from all the shapes and stick them in place on the right-hand side of the cover. Add the orange flower to the outside of the flap.

🖊 White paper, three 14.5 x 21cm (5¾ x 8¼in) pieces 🖊 Lime green foam, A4 sheet
🖊 Plastic jewels 🖊 Velcro dot 🖊 Ballpoint pen 🖊 Basic tool kit (see page 12)

Child's Play

If you find PVA glue too messy, attach the jewels to the butterfly and daisies with glue dots instead.

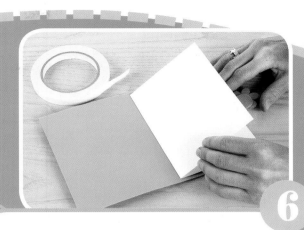

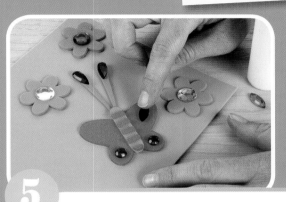

5 Cut two long thin strips of turquoise foam for the butterfly's antennae. Cut thin strips of red foam to make the stripes on the butterfly's back. Stick them all in place. Glue two jewels to each butterfly wing and one in the centre of each flower. Leave to dry.

6 Fold the rectangle of thick white card in half. Place the journal cover face down. Tape the left-hand side of the card to the left-hand inside cover, matching the fold with the crease in the middle of the cover. Apply double-sided tape to the back of the right-hand side of the card, peel off the backing and fold the other half of the cover around it.

Child's Play

When you tape the cover to the card, avoid wrapping it around too tightly or the journal won't close properly afterwards.

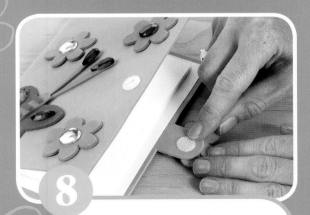

7 To make the pages, fold each piece of white paper in half. Spread a little glue down the fold on two of them. Glue the second sheet inside the first one and the third sheet inside the second one to make a booklet. Stick the booklet in the centre of the back cover of the journal with double-sided tape.

8 Stick one half of a velcro dot to the wrong side of the flap. Fold the flap over and stick the second half directly underneath the first to make a fastening for the journal.

More Fun with Foam

Jurassic journal

This card has a cover made from bright red foam decorated with fun, pre-cut dinosaur shapes.

If you use self-adhesive foam shapes this will be a very quick and easy design to make. The pre-cut shapes were quite large so I customized them with little stripes and spots cut from scraps of leftover foam. I decorated the clasp, a focal point of the card, with a face cut from one of the dinosaur shapes. The blank pages inside the card will make a handy drawing book.

Sock it to 'em

This card has a smart blue, foam jacket and is perfect for sports-mad boys.

I decorated the jacket with baseball stickers and large holographic stars, but you could customize it in lots of other ways, for example with the colours of a school or national team, or with stickers featuring another sport. I filled the journal with graph paper rather than plain sheets to help a child jot down statistics. It could be used to record the progress of a favourite team during the season, with details of games, players and scores.

Hey, cow girl

Foam also comes in animal print designs and I couldn't wait to use this cow-print when I saw it.

I used it to make a rodeo-style journal which I edged with thin strips of red, self-adhesive foam. This looks like whip stitch and gives it an authentic feel teenage girls will love. On the front of the journal is a western-style star with a metal horse charm in the centre. You could also cut up lengths of non-adhesive foam in a contrasting colour to make a fringe to go round the edge of the journal.

Festive jotter

This journal card will be handy for jotting down Christmas lists in the run-up to the festive season and is another quick and easy design to make.

It could even become a mini-scrapbook if your child has a digital camera. Adding a photo of each present beside the name of the person who gave it would make the job of writing thank you letters much easier. The journal is covered with purple foam that contrasts boldly with the green tree. This simple shape is broken up by bands of colour and decorated with self-adhesive jewel embellishments.

Marking the Milestones

These large designs are a fresh take on traditional numbered birthday cards.
The number is still a key element of the design, but it is embellished in lots of fun and unusual ways. On some of the cards the numbers are transformed into a train track or a road, for example, with train or car stickers running around them. On others, the design features carefully decorated numbers. There is plenty of scope for adapting the designs to suit individual children, reflecting their own interests.

An eighteenth birthday card is an important celebration of freedom and maturity with the promise of new horizons ahead. Such an occasion calls for a strong visual statement like Freedom to Roam, opposite, for which I cut a bold number 18 from black and white paper to represent the open road. The cars are made from rub-downs stuck to coloured paper and the card is loosely tied with a tag decorated with two silver horseshoes.

This bold design will make a coming of age card with a difference. The background was cut from an old map – so many roads, so little time!

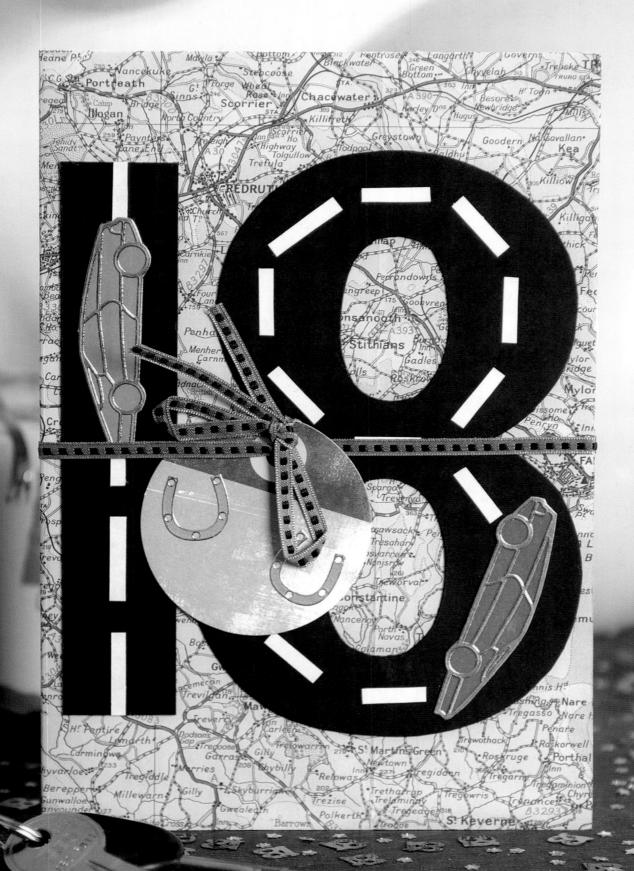

Freedom to Roam

You will need:
✎ Thick white card, 27 x 20cm (5¼ x 8in) ✎ Thin white card
✎ Card tag ✎ Horseshoe stickers
✎ Ribbon, 30cm (12in) length

1 Fold the thick white card in half. Cut a 20 x 16cm (8in x 6¼in) piece from the old map. Glue this to the card front, fold the excess to the back and glue in place (see page 15).

Child's Play

If you're having problems seeing your pencil lines when transferring a template to black paper, use a white pencil crayon so the lines show up clearly.

2 Trace the numbers 1 and 8 from page 105 and transfer them to thin white card to make templates (see page 17). Draw around the templates onto black paper and cut out the numbers.

3 Cut a strip of white paper 4mm (⅛in) wide. Cut it into 15mm (½in) lengths to make road markings. Glue these to each number as shown.

Child's Play

When cutting around stickers, angle the blades of the scissors towards the sticker to help you to cut as close to it as possible.

4 Apply one car sticker to red paper and another one to blue paper. Cut out round the stickers.

✎ Black paper ✎ White paper ✎ Old map ✎ Two gold car stickers
✎ Basic tool kit (see page 12)

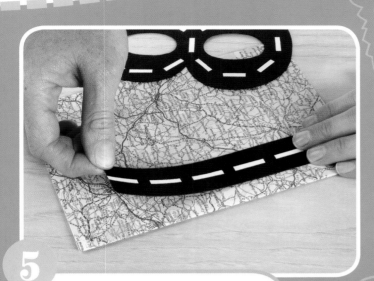

5

Glue the numbers to the front of the card, leaving an equal gap on opposite sides of the card.

6

Glue the cars in place on the numbers to look as though they are driving around them.

7

Press out the tag from the sheet of card. Apply two horseshoe stickers to the tag.

8

Tie the ribbon loosely around the card, attaching the tag at the same time.

More Special Numbers

All aboard!

Knowing how fascinating a train set can be when you're only three, I decided to transform the number 3 on this card into a train track. I added sleepers cut from thin brown card and silver glitter-glue rails.

I applied some train stickers around the edge of the number, which is mounted on foam craft pads for extra dimension. The thin, serrated border, cut with zigzag scissors from a scrap of sparkling red paper, picks up the red from the stickers nicely, and contrasts well with the electric blue background.

First milestone

For this first birthday card, I cut a thick rectangle of pale green card to make a number 1 and decorated it with satin ribbons, rick rack braid and little buttons in subtle shades of lilac, pale green and yellow.

I added a white paper flame above the number to turn it into a birthday candle and attached it to the card with craft pads to add dimension. I chose pastel shades instead of using too much pink or blue to make the design suitable for a boy or a girl.

Budding gardeners

This card is inspired by gardening, an activity that often has a lot of appeal for seven-year-olds.

To highlight the horticultural theme, I cut the number from a leaf patterned scrapbooking paper in soft shades of blue and green. The background is a lime green paper with tiny pale green dots, another scrapbooking find. The earth is represented by lilac paper with a torn edge. The number is placed in the centre of the card as though it has emerged from the ground, surrounded by stamped flowers in soft colours. As a fun finishing touch, stamped insects busily tend the make-believe garden..

All glammed up

I designed this card with my glamorous 15-year-old niece and her friends in mind. I made a shimmering lipstick case from pink paper topped with silver holographic paper in the shape of a number 1, and cut a number 5 from striped paper and decorated it with shiny rhinestones.

The lower section of the card is covered with a bubble patterned scrapbooking paper. Mounted on top are three tags stamped with shoes, handbags and flowers in the style of the drawings in French fashion magazines. The tags are held in place by lilac eyelets, and look like the clothing tags you find in an expensive boutique.

Child's Play
See pages 98–99 for the templates to make these special-number cards.

Garlands Galore

Children love folded cards, especially when they're cut into fun shapes and decorated with glitter and embellishments. All the designs in this chapter are made from a single folded sheet that is cut out as one piece like a paper dolly and opened out to make a garland. I used an A4 sheet of card for each one, making them quick and easy cards to produce.

The gleeful skeletons in the main design Funny Bones, opposite, are perfect for a Halloween party invitation. They were cut from a sheet of thick card, then covered in a deep layer of pure white glitter. Their eyes are created with two large red sequins and their bones are defined with purple glitter glue. The rest of their bodies are highlighted with flashes of silver glitter glue.

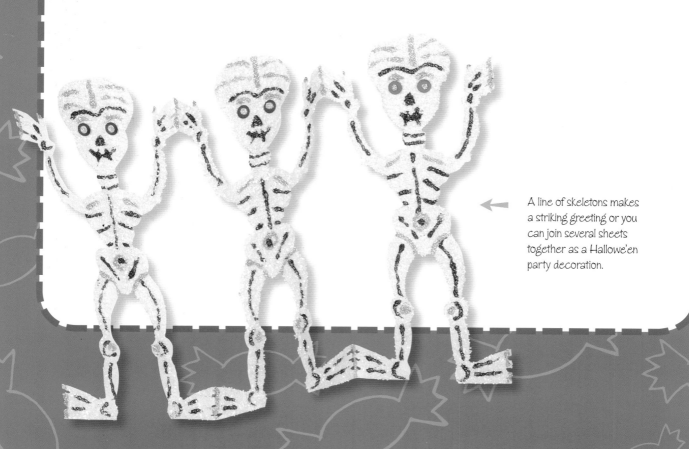

A line of skeletons makes a striking greeting or you can join several sheets together as a Hallowe'en party decoration.

Funny Bones

You will need:

✎ Thick white card, A4 sheet ✎ Scrap paper ✎ White glitter

1 Divide the card into three equal sections. Fold the first third over, turn the card face down and fold the other third over to make a concertina (see page 14).

Child's Play

When transferring the skeleton pattern, make sure the skeleton's hands and feet extend right up to the folds, to ensure the three skeletons join up when the card is opened.

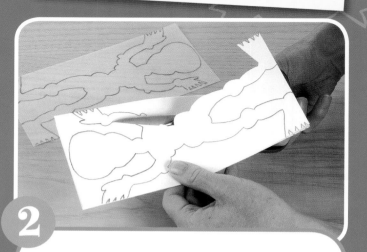

2 Trace the skeleton template from page 109. Transfer this image to the top fold of the concertina (see page 17). Hold all the sections of the card firmly together and cut out the skeleton.

Open out the garland and place it face up on a sheet of scrap paper. Spread PVA glue all over it.

3

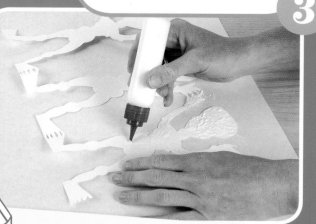

Child's Play

Spread the PVA glue over the garland as smoothly as possible to ensure the glitter has a nice flat surface.

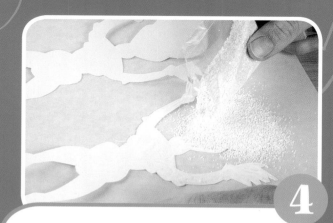

4 Sprinkle a generous layer of white glitter over the skeletons and leave for a bout 10 minutes to set slightly. Pour off the excess glitter.

5 Squeeze two dots of PVA glue on to each skull in the eye positions and attach a red sequin for each eye.

6 Draw a nose and mouth on each skeleton with purple glitter glue.

7 Draw the bones on each skeleton with purple glitter glue, using the photograph as a guide.

8 Add dots of silver glitter glue to the end of each skeleton's fingers and toes. Add more touches of silver where desired.

More Gorgeous Garlands

Going cheep!

Little children love baby animals and they also enjoy the element of surprise you can create with a folding card.

This chick garland will make a super Easter card for tots. The chicks are joined at the beak and tummy, and are standing on a patch of grass cut from bright green paper with zigzag scissors. The grass is strewn with little daisies punched from white paper, which have pink centres made using a round punch. The chicks have beaks and wings cut from orange paper and their eyes are dotted in with a very fine, black marker pen.

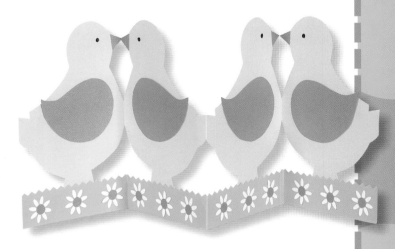

Defenders of the universe

Here's a fun, folding card to make for a boy. This funky robot is cut from mirror card and decorated with scraps of self-adhesive holographic paper and stickers.

You can have great fun adding materials you already have to create the right effect on a garland. I used punched dots and shiny paper stars to make my robots look cool and efficient. I gave them a bright yellow, sparkling instrument panel decorated with tiny holographic stars. I divided up their arms and legs with thin strips of paper, and made eyes from circles of holographic card and small daisy stickers.

Flower power

I chose metallic self-adhesive paper in four bright colours to make this bold and funky daisy garland card teenage girls will love.

I cut the daisy shapes from a folded sheet of pink metallic paper stuck to card. I then attached orange petals to half of the daisies. I added an orange and a turquoise circle in the centre of each daisy and decorated them with different coloured punched dots.

Sugar and spice

Children will love this variation on a traditional Christmas treat – a garland of cute little gingerbread figures, including gingerbread boys and gingerbread girls!

I used a bronze pearlescent base card rather than a plain brown one because it looks nice and festive. The clothes are decorated with frosty patterns drawn with silver glitter glue and buttons and pom poms created from paper stickers. I punched circles from black paper for their eyes. The gingerbread girl has a snowflake punched from silver holographic paper on her pink beret.

Child's Play

See pages 106–107 for the templates to make these garland cards.

Cut It Out

Large-scale cards have plenty of visual impact and make a strong focal point when displayed in a room. All the cards in this chapter have a large central image that shows at a glance what the subject of the card is. Down the left-hand side are three smaller tags that expand on this theme. Tags are an ideal way of adding textural interest to a card and can be decorated with favourite papers and embellishments that mean something to you or the recipient.

Winner's Trophy, opposite, has a large trophy cut from silver mirror card as its central image and a green background that resembles the turf of a playing field. A shield cut from gold card is attached to the trophy with stylish metal snap fasteners. You could also personalize it with a message or the recipient's name using rub-down letters. Each tag has a silver rub-down on a football theme and is pushed into a pocket made from a retro-style card tag.

This trophy card is perfect for a keen sports fan who dreams of playing for their country one day.

Winner's Trophy

You will need:

✎ Thick silver card, A4 sheet ✎ Thin silver mirror card, A4 sheet ✎ Small white tags, three ✎ Retro-style pre-printed card tags ✎ 3mm pale aqua satin ribbon, 30cm (12in) ✎ Eyelet punch

Child's Play

Use a craft knife to cut out small fiddly, enclosed areas such as the inside of the trophy handles.

1 Fold the sheet of silver card in half. Glue the green paper to the front of the card, lining up the right hand edge on each piece.

2 Trace the trophy from page 108. Redraw over the lines to transfer the image onto the silver mirror card (see page 17). Transfer the shield onto gold paper. Cut them both out.

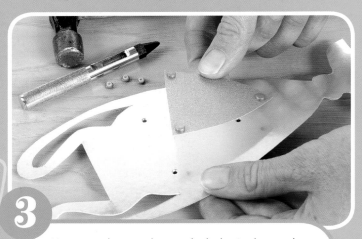

3 Use an eyelet punch to make holes in the trophy and shield where marked. Attach the plaque to the front of the trophy with silver snap fasteners.

Child's Play

If you can't find silver snap fasteners to attach the plaque to the trophy, silver eyelets are just as suitable.

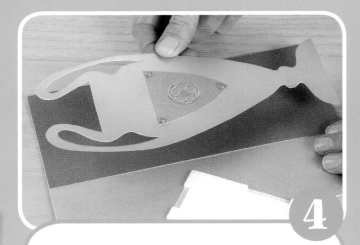

4 Apply a silver football rub-down sticker to the middle of the shield. Add craft pads to the back of the trophy and attach it to the green background, leaving equal space on either side of the handles.

✎ Thin gold card, small piece ✎ Thin blue card ✎ Green paper, 9 x 21cm (3½ x 8¼in)
✎ Silver football rub-down stickers ✎ Silver snap fasteners ✎ Silver snap fasteners
✎ Basic tool kit (see page 12)

Child's Play
For quick and easy tags try using one of the paper punches or die-cutting tools that produce tags in a range of different sizes.

5

To make the blue tags, glue three plain white tags to thin blue card. When the glue is dry, carefully cut out the tags. Working on the front of each tag, re-make the holes with the eyelet punch (see page 16).

6

Apply either a silver footballer or a football rub-down sticker to the front of each tag.

7

Press out three squares from the sheet of card tags. Decorate each one with more squares or circles from the sheet. Apply a thin line of glue around the sides and bottom of each square. Glue them on down the left side of the card to make pockets. Leave to dry thoroughly.

8

Cut three, 10cm (4in) lengths of aqua ribbon. Tie a piece of ribbon through the hole in the top of each tag. Insert a tag into each pocket.

More Shapes to Cut Out

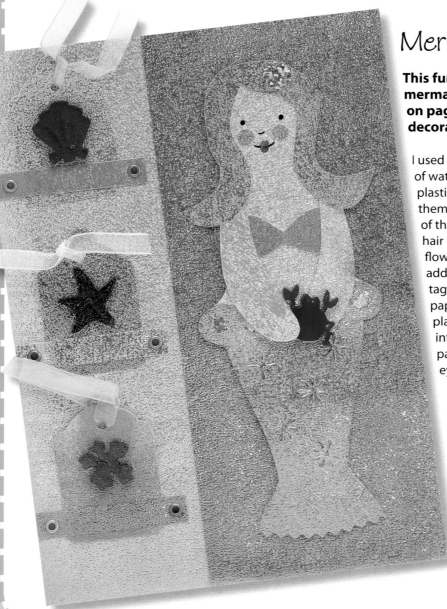

Merry mermaid

This fun seaside card features a mermaid cut from the templates on page 109 and three matching decorated tags.

I used iridescent paper in a selection of watery shades and some fun plastic embellishments on a seaside theme. The mermaid is holding one of these, a red crab, in her arms. Her hair is decorated with a sparkling flower sticker and her features are added with fine marker pens. The tags are covered with iridescent paper and embellished with the plastic shapes. Each tag is slotted into a carrier or thin strip of paper held in place with metallic eyelets (see page 16).

Clear round

A large rosette cut from the template on page 110 is the central image on this card to celebrate sporting success at the gymkhana.

I made this design from plain and patterned scrapbooking paper and added a photo sticker of a pony in the centre. The tags are covered with coordinating coloured paper and an appropriate sticker for the occasion. Each tag is slotted into a slit cut directly into the card, and finished off with a ribbon tie.

Child's Play

See page 12 for tips on cutting out the perfect templates.

Templates

All templates are full size, ready to be traced or photocopied.

Vampire Greetings, page 43

Friendly Rudolf, page 43

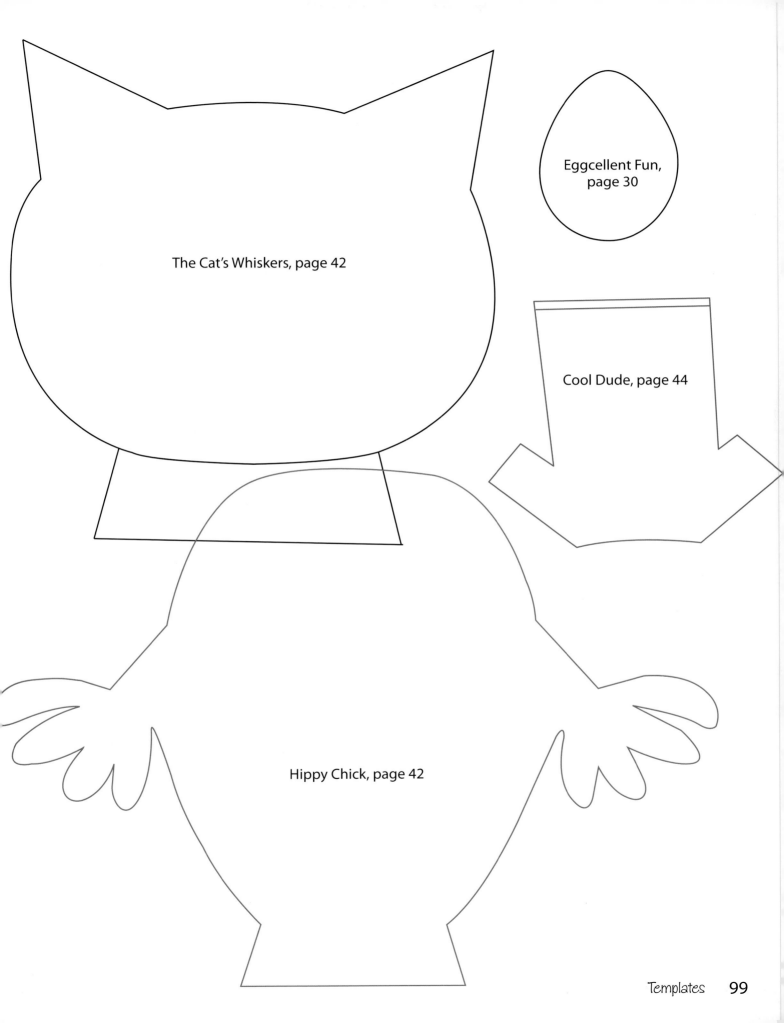

Eggcellent Fun, page 30

The Cat's Whiskers, page 42

Cool Dude, page 44

Hippy Chick, page 42

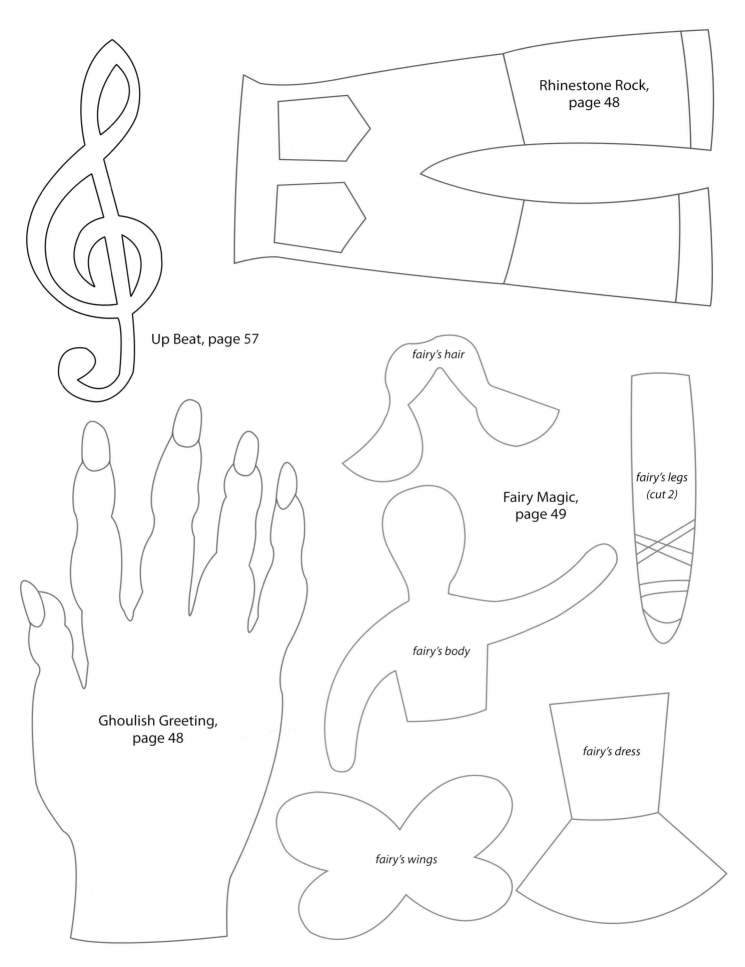

Rhinestone Rock,
page 48

Up Beat, page 57

fairy's hair

Fairy Magic,
page 49

*fairy's legs
(cut 2)*

fairy's body

Ghoulish Greeting,
page 48

fairy's dress

fairy's wings

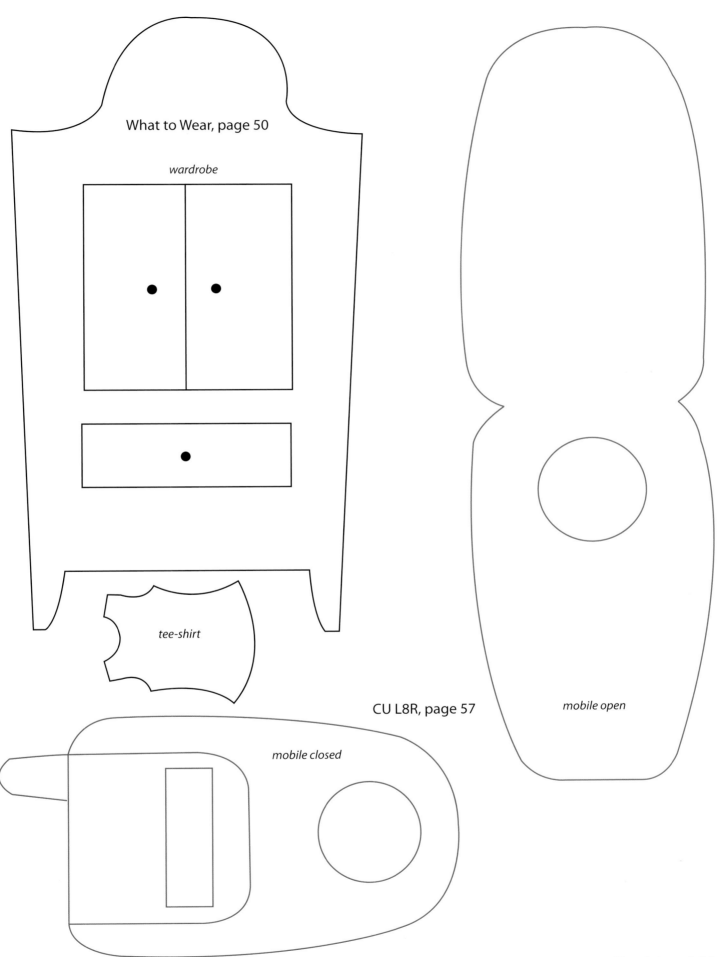

What to Wear, page 50

wardrobe

tee-shirt

CU L8R, page 57

mobile open

mobile closed

Jolly Snowman, page 60

cracker

snowman's hat and scarf

snowman's body

Swan Lake, page 64

snowman shaker frame

Halloween Horrors,
page 64

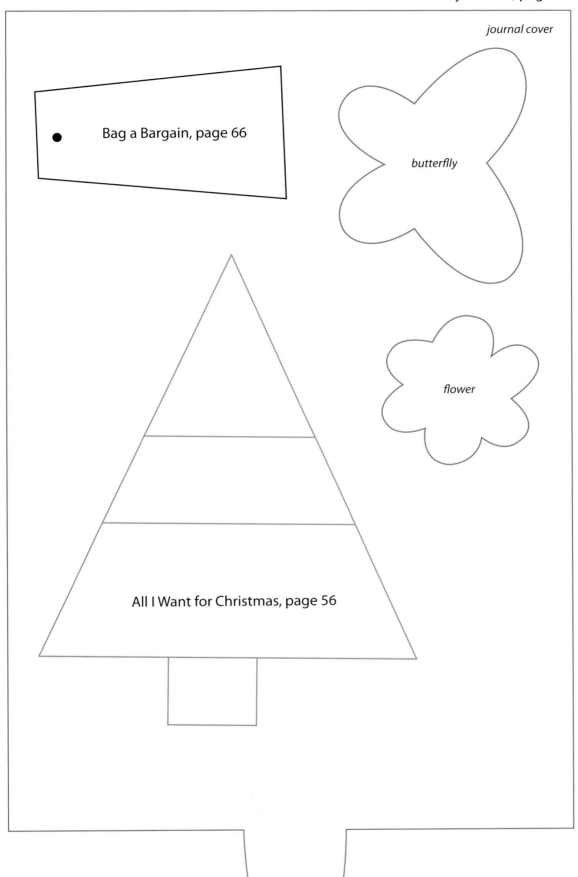

journal cover

Bag a Bargain, page 66

butterflly

flower

All I Want for Christmas, page 56

All Glammed Up, page 85

All Aboard, page 84

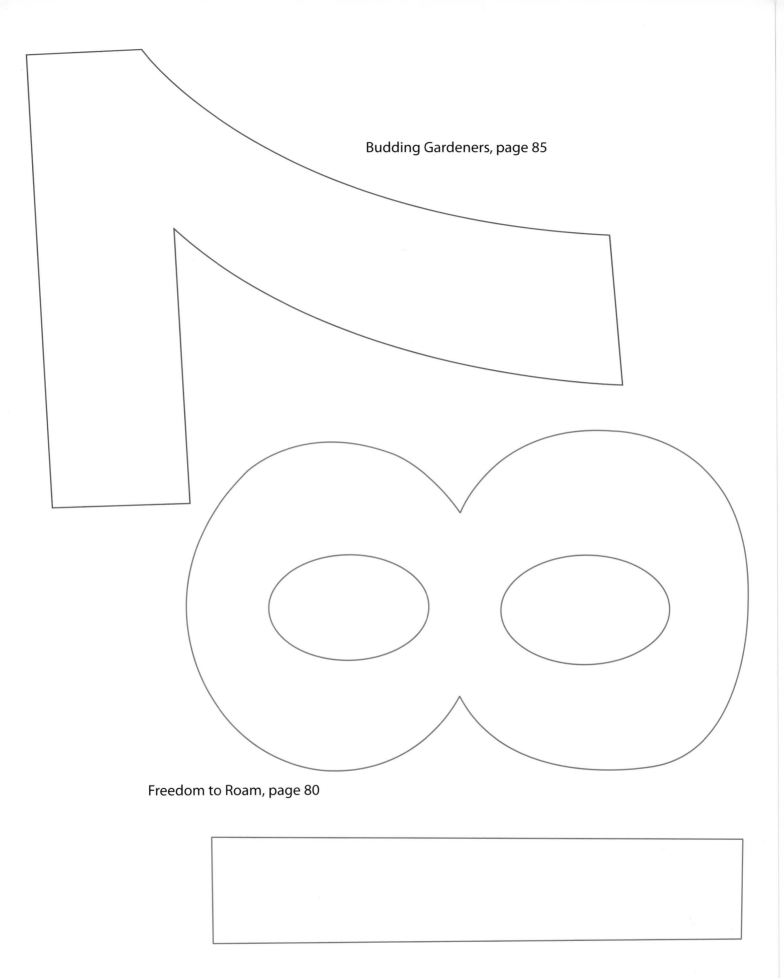

Budding Gardeners, page 85

Freedom to Roam, page 80

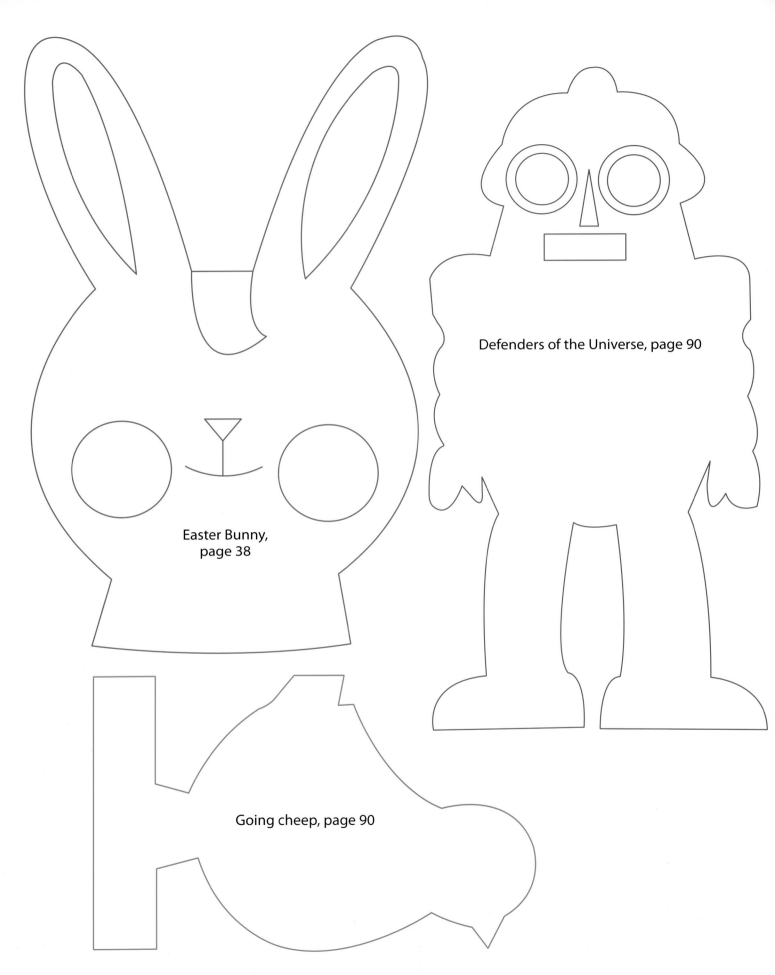

Defenders of the Universe, page 90

Easter Bunny,
page 38

Going cheep, page 90

gingerbread trousers

gingerbread skirt

Sugar and Spice, page 91

gingerbread body

gingerbread beret

gingerbread hat

Flower power, page 91

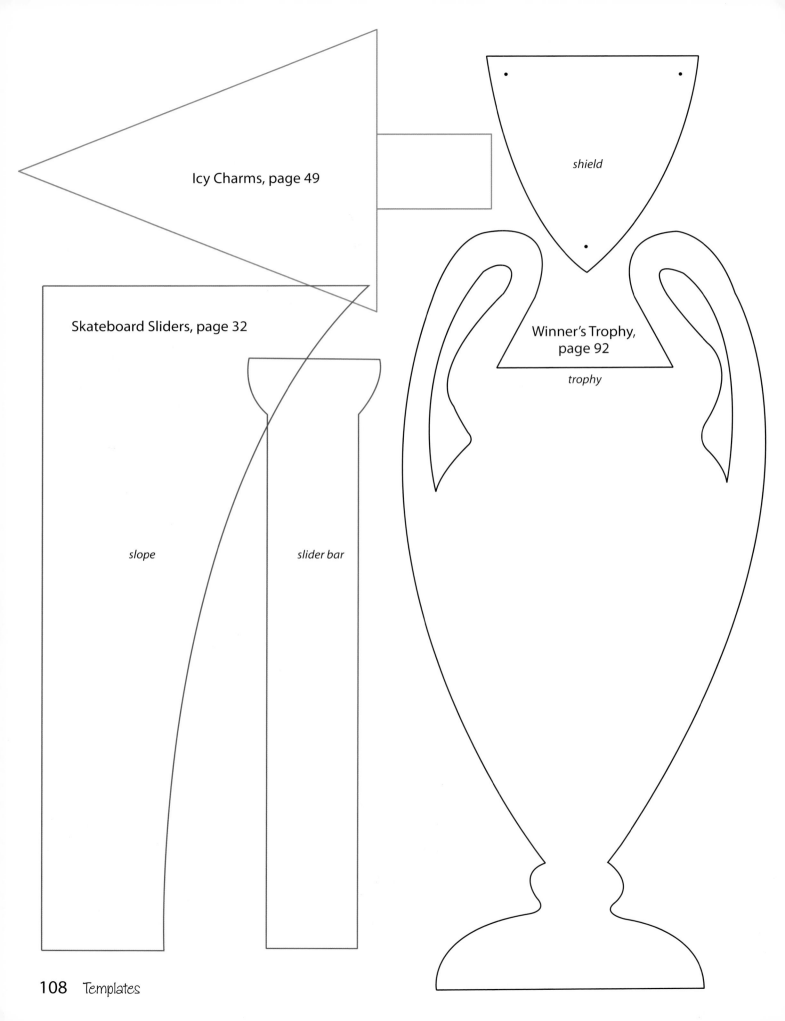

Icy Charms, page 49

Skateboard Sliders, page 32

slope

slider bar

shield

Winner's Trophy,
page 92

trophy

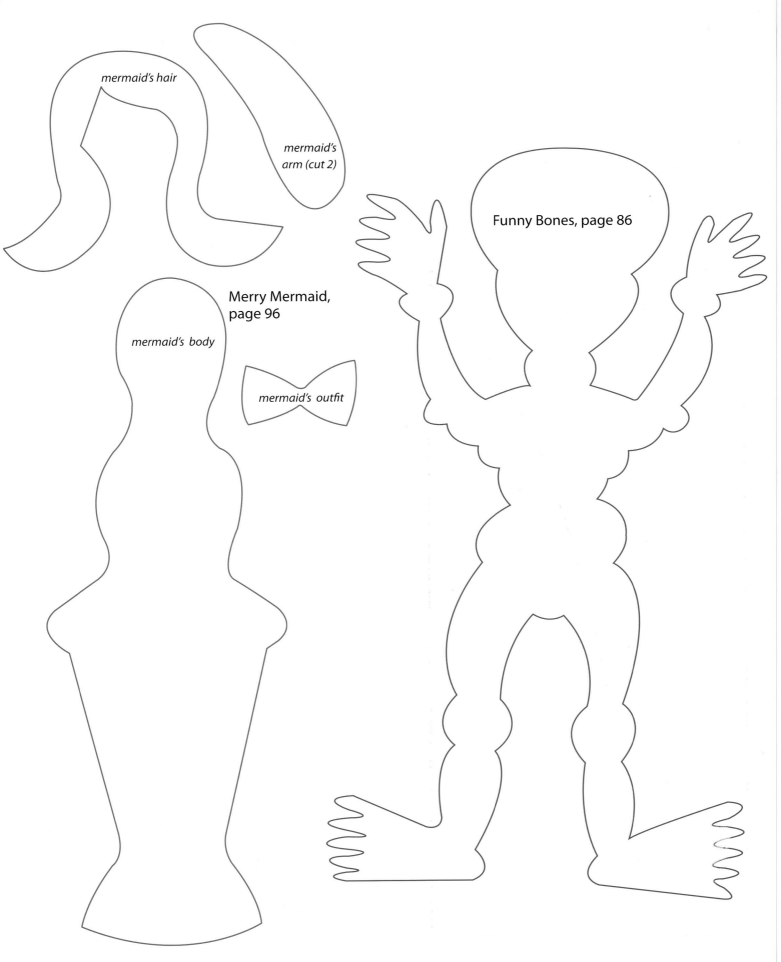

mermaid's hair

mermaid's arm (cut 2)

Funny Bones, page 86

Merry Mermaid, page 96

mermaid's body

mermaid's outfit

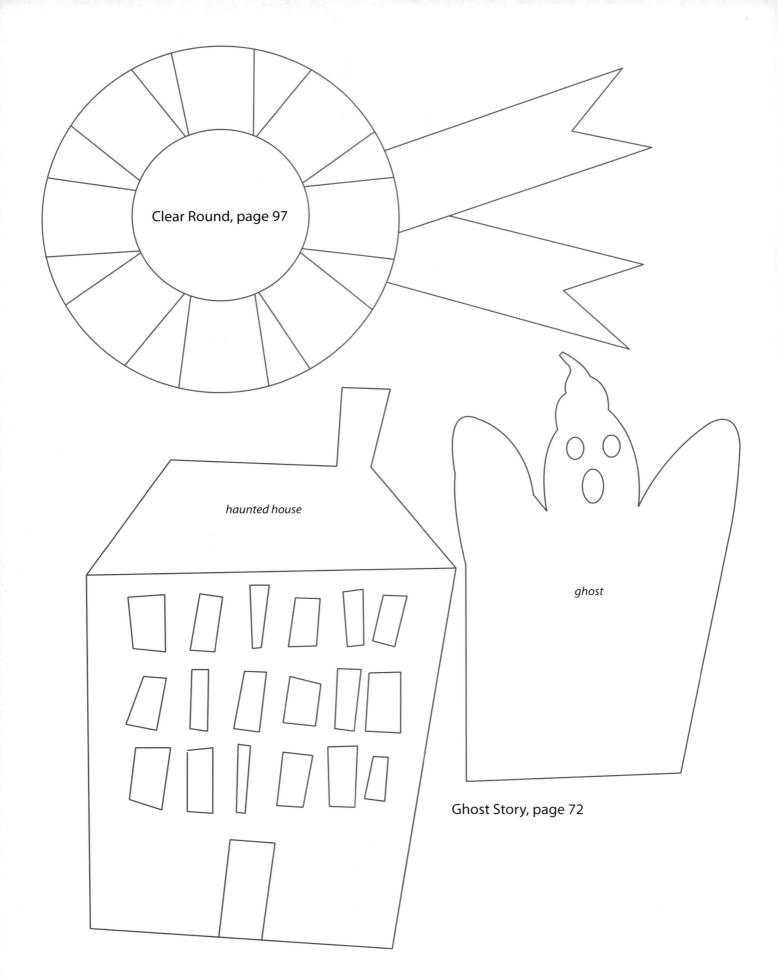

Clear Round, page 97

haunted house

ghost

Ghost Story, page 72

Every effort has been made to trace the suppliers of materials used. The following information is correct at the time of going to press, but details are unavoidably subject to change.

Materials

Concertina Keepsakes

My First Year
Pink gingham paper: Pebbles Inc (Scrap Genie)
Paper ribbon sticker: Pebbles Inc (Scrap Genie)
Pink twine (I kandee twine, pastels): Pebbles Inc (Scrap Genie)
Daisy, bib, pin, flower and photo stickers: Pebbles Inc (Simply Create)
Flower stickers: L'il Davis (Scrap Genie)
Self adhesive ribbon: Anita's (DoCrafts)

On the Road
Car stamp: Funstamps
Car stickers: Z Design (Avery Dennison Zweckform)

Birthday Surprise
Animal/candle stickers: Pebbles Inc (Scrap Genie)
Scrapbooking papers: Basic Grey (Scrap Genie)

Pocketful of Memories

Starting School
Pencil and boy stamps: DoCrafts
Ruler and pencil charms: Favorite Findings (Habico)
Number/letter stickers: Pebbles Inc. (Scrap Genie)
Frame: My Boy Mod Blox by Ki Memories
Green ringlets by Scrapworks
Number dots: alphadotz by Scrapworks
Silver rings: hugz by Scrapworks
Paper fasteners: primary mini circles by Making Memories
Photo stickers: Pebbles Inc (Scrap Genie)

Naming Day
Paper: Simply Create
Photo stickers: Pebbles Inc (Scrap Genie)

Girlfriends for Ever
Flowery paper: American Crafts (Simply Create)
Gingham Paper: Pebbles Inc (Scrap Genie)
Embellishments: Habico

Countdown to Christmas
Stickers: Mrs Grossman's Paper Co (Simply Create)
Charms: Heidi Grace Designs
Number rubdowns: Simply Create
Paper: American crafts (Simply Create)

Eggcellent Fun
Scrapbooking papers: American Crafts (Simply Create)

Watch Them Move

Skateboarders
Stickers: Woolworths

Peekaboo
Duck and daisy stickers: Pebbles Inc (Scrap Genie)
Gingham paper: Pebbles Inc (Scrap Genie)

Party Night
Girly stickers: Z Design (Avery Dennison Zweckform)

Joggle-Eye Fun

Hippy chick
Flower stickers: Stickopotamus by EK Success (www.eksuccess.com)

Embellished with Style

Cool Dude
Camouflage paper: Making Memories
Star brads: Avec BV
Tag: My Guy Mod Blox by Ki Memories
Silver hugz: Scrapworks
Number alphadotz: Scrapworks

Ghoulish Greeting
Spider: Hallowe'en Mix by Heidi Grace designs
Pumpkin stickers: Mrs Grossman's Paper Co (Simply Create)
Stripy paper: Pixie Press

Rhinestone Rock
Heart charm: Craftime Ltd
Vellum heart stickers: Mrs Grossman's Paper Co (Simply Create)
Denim sticker: Mrs Grossman's Paper Co (Simply Create)

Icy Charms
Charm: Craftime Ltd
Ribbon: Making Memories
Snowflake punch: Habico
Spotted paper: Simply Create

Fairy Magic
Nylon butterfly: Craftime

Lift the Flaps

What to Wear
Spotted paper: American Crafts (Simply Create)
Paper inside wardrobe: Bella Press
Coat hanger: Impex
Daisy stamp: Do Crafts
Pink paper: Pebbles Inc (Scrap Genie)
Daisy punch: Habico

All Tied Up
Denim sticker: Mrs Grossman's Paper Co (Simply Create)
Number stickers: Pebbles Inc (Scrap Genie)
Green ringlets: Scrapworks

All I want for Christmas
Star sticker: Doodlebug design

Up Beat
Striped paper: American Crafts (Simply Create)

C U L8R
Stamp: Woodware Craft Collection
Smiley stickers: Woolworths

Shake It Up

Jolly Snowman
Green dotted scrapbooking paper: Scrapbook House
Snowflake punch: Habico

Swan Lake
Striped scrapbooking paper: American Crafts (Simply Create)
Stickers: Z Design (Avery Dennison Zweckform)

Snowdome Shaker
Funky foam: DoCrafts

Hallowe'en Horrors

Spider scrapbooking paper: Making Memories
Spider confetti: Creativity International Ltd

Key to the Door
Frame: Pebbles Inc (Scrap Genie)
18 confetti: Unique Ind. Inc
Paper: American Crafts (Simply Create)

Token of Appreciation

Bag a Bargain
Lime green dotted paper: American Crafts (Simply Create)
Heart punch: Habico
Daisy punch: Habico
Stamp: Woodware Crafts

Ghost Story
Paper: Basic Grey (Scrap Genie)

Retail Therapy
Pocket sticker: Mrs Grossman's Paper Co (Simply Create)
Ribbon: Making Memories
Safety pins: Making Memories
Paper on tags: Bella press
Gingham paper: Simply Create

Precious Gift
Stickers: L'il Davis (Scrap Genie)
Heart punch: Habico

Accessorize
Vellum dots and hearts: Mrs Grossman's Paper Co (Simply Create)
Envelopes: Card Art
Ribbon: Making Memories

Funky Foam Journals

Funky Garden
Foam sheet: DoCrafts

Jurassic journal
Foam sheet: DoCrafts
Foam dinos: Craftime Ltd

Sock It to 'em
Foam sheet: DoCrafts
Stickers: Mrs Grossman's Paper Co (Simply Create)

Hey, Cow Girl
Animal print foam sheet: Craftime Ltd
Horse charm: Craftime Ltd

Festive Jotter
Foam sheet: DoCrafts
Self-adhesive jewels: Craftime Ltd

Marking the Milestones

Freedom to Roam
Car and horseshoe rub-downs: Habico
Tag: Basic Grey (Scrap Genie)
Ribbon: Making memories

All Aboard!
Stickers: Mrs Grossman's Paper Co (Simply Create)

Budding Gardeners
Insect and flower stamps: Woodware

All Glammed Up
Tag and shoe stamps: Woodware
Scrapbooking paper: American Crafts (Simply Create)

Garlands Galore

Defenders of the Universe
Daisy stickers: Habico

Cut It Out

Winner's Trophy
Tags: My Guy Mod Blox (Ki Memories)
Football rub-downs: Habico

Merry Mermaid
Glass effect charms: Heidi Grace Designs
Daisy stickers: Habico

Clear Round
Paper: Simply Create
Pony sticker: Z Design (Avery Dennison Zweckform)
Trophy /rosette/medal stickers: Mrs Grossman's Paper Co (Simply Create)

Acknowledgments

I would like to thank the following suppliers and manufacturers who agreed to give materials to be used in this book, your generosity is greatly appreciated.

Kate Garnett at The Scrapbook House, Becks Fagg and Debbie Stewart at Scrapgenie, Rachel Boxhall at Habico, Judith at Woodware, Emma Buckingham at DoCrafts, and Mark Catron at Craft Time.

Love and thanks as ever to Neil and Stella for their patience and understanding, and to Bill, Sylvia and Sandra Hadfield for extra special child care! Thank you to Joe and Annie Heap for letting me use their lovely photo s. I would also like to thank Cheryl Brown for her enthusiastic response to a rather hazy idea, and for support all the way through, to Karl Adamson for photography, Jenny Proverbs for pushing it all through and Juliet Bracken for her immaculate copy editing.

Suppliers

UK and Europe

Avec BV
www.avec-creative.nl

Avery Dennison Zweckform
Postfach 1252
D - 83602 Holzkirchen
www.sticker.de

Card Art
www.cardart.co.uk

Craftime Ltd
Unit 15, Hazelford Way
Industrial Estate, Newstead,
Nottinghamshire NG15 0DG
tel: 08707-577622
www.craftime.com

Creativity International Ltd
www.cilimited.co.uk

DoCrafts
www.docrafts.co.uk
tel: 01202 811000

Habico
Tong Road industrial estate
Amberley Road
Leeds LS12 4BD
tel: 0113-263-1500
www.habico.co.uk

Impex Creative Crafts Ltd
Impex House, Atlas Road
Wembley, Middlesex HA9 0TX
www.impexcreativecrafts.co.uk

Scrap Genie
tel: 01440-704400
www.scrapgenie.co.uk

Simply Create
The Square, Stow on the Wold
Gloucestershire GL54 1AF
tel: 01451 833547
www.thescrapbookhouse.com

Woodware Craft Collection
Unit 2A, Sandylands
Business Park, Skipton
North Yorkshire BD23 2DE
tel: 01756-700024
sales@woodware.co.uk

US Suppliers

American Crafts
tel: 800-879-5185
acsales@americancrafts.com

Basic Grey
1343 Flint Meadow Drive #6
Kaysville, Utah 84037
Tel: 801-544-1116

Bella Press
www.bellapress.com

Doodlebug Design Inc
tel: 801-952-0555

EK Success
www.eksuccess.com

Heidi Grace Designs
www.heidigrace.com

Junkitz
tel: 732-792-1108
www.junkitz.com

Ki Memories
www.kimemories.com

L'il Davis
17835 Sky Park Circle,
Suite C, Irvine CA 92614
tel: 949-838-0344

Making Memories
tel: 800-286-5263
www.makingmemories.com

Mrs Grossman's Paper Company
PO Box 4467
Petaluma CA 94955
tel: 800-429-4549
www.mrsgrossmans.com

Pebbles Inc
1132 South State Street
Orem Ut 84097
tel: 801-235-1520
www.pebblesinc.com

Pixie Press
Darice Inc, 13000 Darice Parkway
Park 82, Strongville, OH 44149
tel: 1-866-432-7423

Sandylion
tel: 1-800-552-4704
www.sandylion.com

Scrapworks
tel: 801-363-1010
www.scrapworks.com

Index

About the author

Marion Elliot is an artist and designer working in a variety of media, especially paper – she has made her own cards for several years and regularly designs ranges for Hallmark. Marion is the author of many craft and design books, and has made TV appearances. She lives in Ludlow, Shropshire.